New York City Edition
Science

Arctic Fox

SCHOOL PUBLISHERS

Visit the Learning Site!
www.harcourtschool.com

Copyright © by Harcourt, Inc.
2008 Edition

All rights reserved. No part of this publication may be reproduced or transmitted in any form or by any means, electronic or mechanical, including photocopy, recording, or any information storage and retrieval system, without permission in writing from the publisher.

Requests for permission to make copies of any part of the work should be addressed to School Permissions and Copyrights, Harcourt, Inc., 6277 Sea Harbor Drive, Orlando, Florida 32887-6777. Fax: 407-345-2418.

HARCOURT and the Harcourt Logo are trademarks of Harcourt, Inc., registered in the United States of America and/or other jurisdictions.

Printed in the United States of America

ISBN 13: 978-0-15-381368-9
ISBN 10: 0-15-381368-7

1 2 3 4 5 6 7 8 9 10   0868   18 17 16 15 14 13 12 11 10 09

Arctic Fox

If you have received these materials as examination copies free of charge, Harcourt School Publishers retains title to the materials and they may not be resold. Resale of examination copies is strictly prohibited and is illegal.

Possession of this publication in print format does not entitle users to convert this publication, or any portion of it, into electronic format.

Consulting Authors

Michael J. Bell
Associate Professor of Early Childhood Education
College of Education
West Chester University of Pennsylvania

Michael A. DiSpezio
Curriculum Architect
JASON Academy
Cape Cod, Massachusetts

Marjorie Frank
Former Adjunct, Science Education
Hunter College
New York, New York

Gerald H. Krockover
Professor of Earth and Atmospheric Science Education
Purdue University
West Lafayette, Indiana

Joyce C. McLeod
Adjunct Professor
Rollins College
Winter Park, Florida

Barbara ten Brink
Science Specialist
Austin Independent School District
Austin, Texas

Carol J. Valenta
Senior Vice President
St. Louis Science Center
St. Louis, Missouri

Barry A. Van Deman
President and CEO
Museum of Life and Science
Durham, North Carolina

Dear Students,

What's special about this Science textbook? It has been specially printed just for students in New York City. Inside you will put your hands on exciting Science Investigations and your minds on engaging science content! You will find special features like Science Spin from Weekly Reader and lots of links to online exploration.

Using this special book will help ensure that you are meeting the Major Understandings in the New York State Science Core Curriculum and the New York City Scope and Sequence. This is because the book includes only the content that matches with the Science Scope and Sequence for New York City. You and your classmates can easily focus on those science topics that are required by the New York City Department of Education.

We hope that you have a successful and exciting year in SCIENCE!

Sincerely,
Harcourt School Publishers

CONTENTS

Ready, Set, Science!   viii

Lesson 1 How Do We Use Our Senses?   2
Lesson 2 How Do We Use Inquiry Skills?   8
Lesson 3 How Do We Use Science Tools?   18
Chapter Review and Test Preparation   24

UNIT 1 Animal Diversity
How are animals alike and different?

Chapter 1   All About Animals   28

Lesson 1 What Are Living and Nonliving Things?   30
Lesson 2 What Do Animals Need?   36
Lesson 3 How Can We Group Animals?   42
Lesson 4 How Do Animals Grow and Change?   50
Chapter Review and Test Preparation   62

Science Spin Weekly Reader
Technology Traveling Turtles   58
People Feeding Time   60

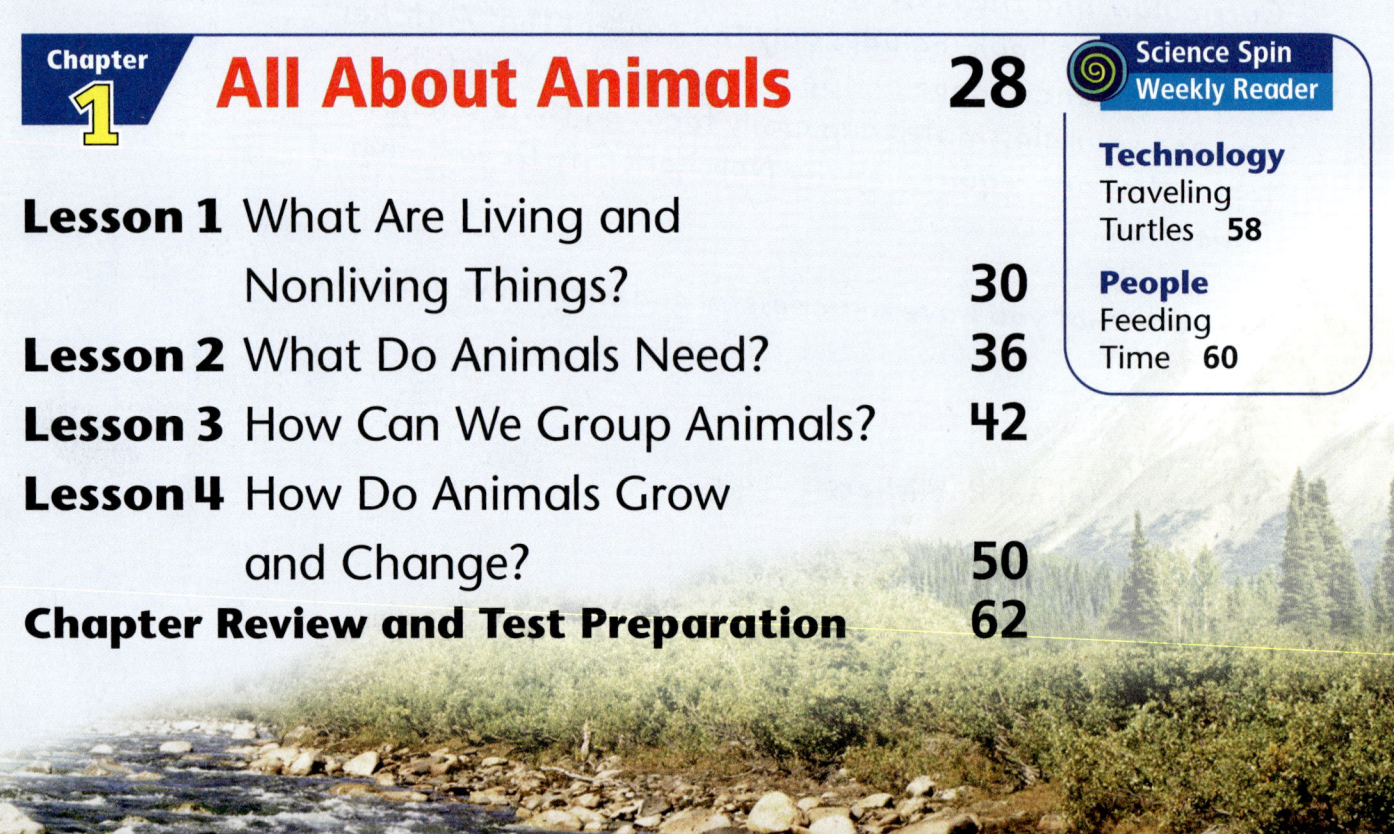

Chapter 2 Environments for Living Things — 64

Lesson 1 What Is an Environment? — 66
Lesson 2 What Helps Plants and Animals Live in Places? — 72
Lesson 3 How Do Plants and Animals Need Each Other? — 80
Chapter Review and Test Preparation — 92

Science Spin Weekly Reader
Technology Now You See It, Now You Don't — 88
People Where Are All the Butterflies? — 90

UNIT 2 Properties of Matter
What are some properties of solids, liquids, and gases?

Chapter 3 All About Matter — 96

Lesson 1 What Is Matter? — 98
Lesson 2 What Can We Observe About Solids? — 104
Lesson 3 What Can We Observe About Liquids? — 112
Lesson 4 What Can We Observe About Gases? — 120
Chapter Review and Test Preparation — 132

Science Spin Weekly Reader
Technology Cleaning Up Oil — 128
People Making Protective Packages — 130

v

Enrichment Chapter

Chapter 4 — Heat, Light, and Sound — 134

Lesson 1 What Is Heat? — 136
Lesson 2 What Can Light Do? — 142
Lesson 3 What Is Sound? — 148
Chapter Review and Test Preparation — 160

Science Spin Weekly Reader
Technology How Cell Phones Work — 156
People Lighting the World — 158

UNIT 3 Weather and Seasons
What are some of the changes we notice between seasons?

Chapter 5 — Measuring Weather — 164

Lesson 1 What Is Weather? — 166
Lesson 2 How Can We Measure Weather? — 172
Lesson 3 What Makes Clouds and Rain? — 178
Chapter Review and Test Preparation — 188

Science Spin Weekly Reader
Technology Is the Weather Getting Worse? — 184
People Watching the Weather — 186

Chapter 6 — Seasons — 190

Lesson 1 What Is Spring? — 192
Lesson 2 What Is Summer? — 200
Lesson 3 What Is Fall? — 206
Lesson 4 What Is Winter? — 212
Chapter Review and Test Preparation — 222

Science Spin Weekly Reader
Technology Snow Is Useful — 218
People Meet Ivy the Inventor — 220

Chapter 7 — Objects in the Sky — 224

Science Spin Weekly Reader
Technology Smart Spacesuits 244
People Studying Mars 246

Lesson 1 What Can We See in the Sky? — 226
Lesson 2 What Causes Day and Night? — 232
Lesson 3 What Can We Observe About the Moon? — 238
Chapter Review and Test Preparation — 248

References — 250

Health Handbook — R1
Reading in Science Handbook — R14
Math in Science Handbook — R20
Safety in Science — R26
Glossary — R27
Index — R45

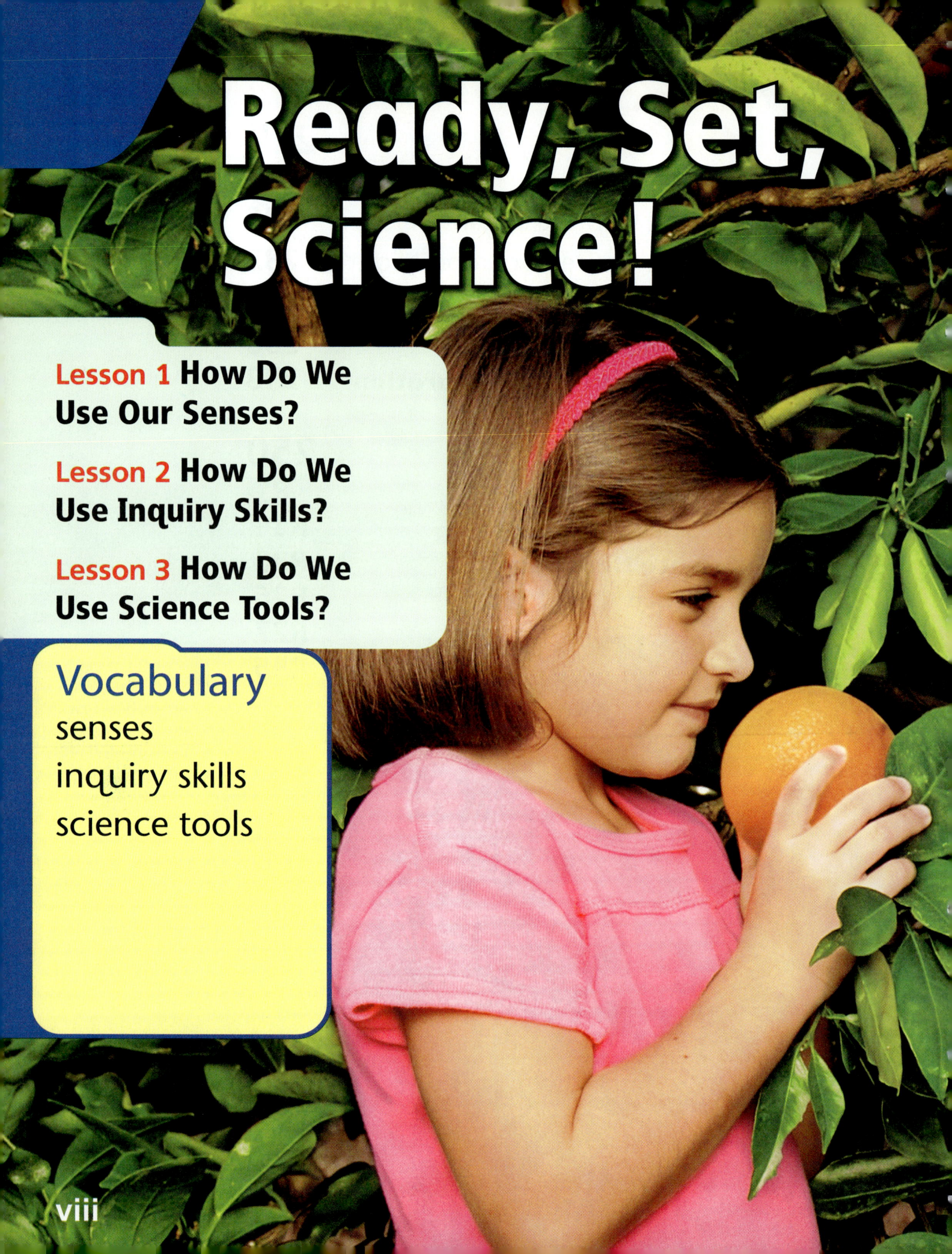

Ready, Set, Science!

Lesson 1 How Do We Use Our Senses?

Lesson 2 How Do We Use Inquiry Skills?

Lesson 3 How Do We Use Science Tools?

Vocabulary
senses
inquiry skills
science tools

I wonder...
Can kids be scientists?

What do you wonder?

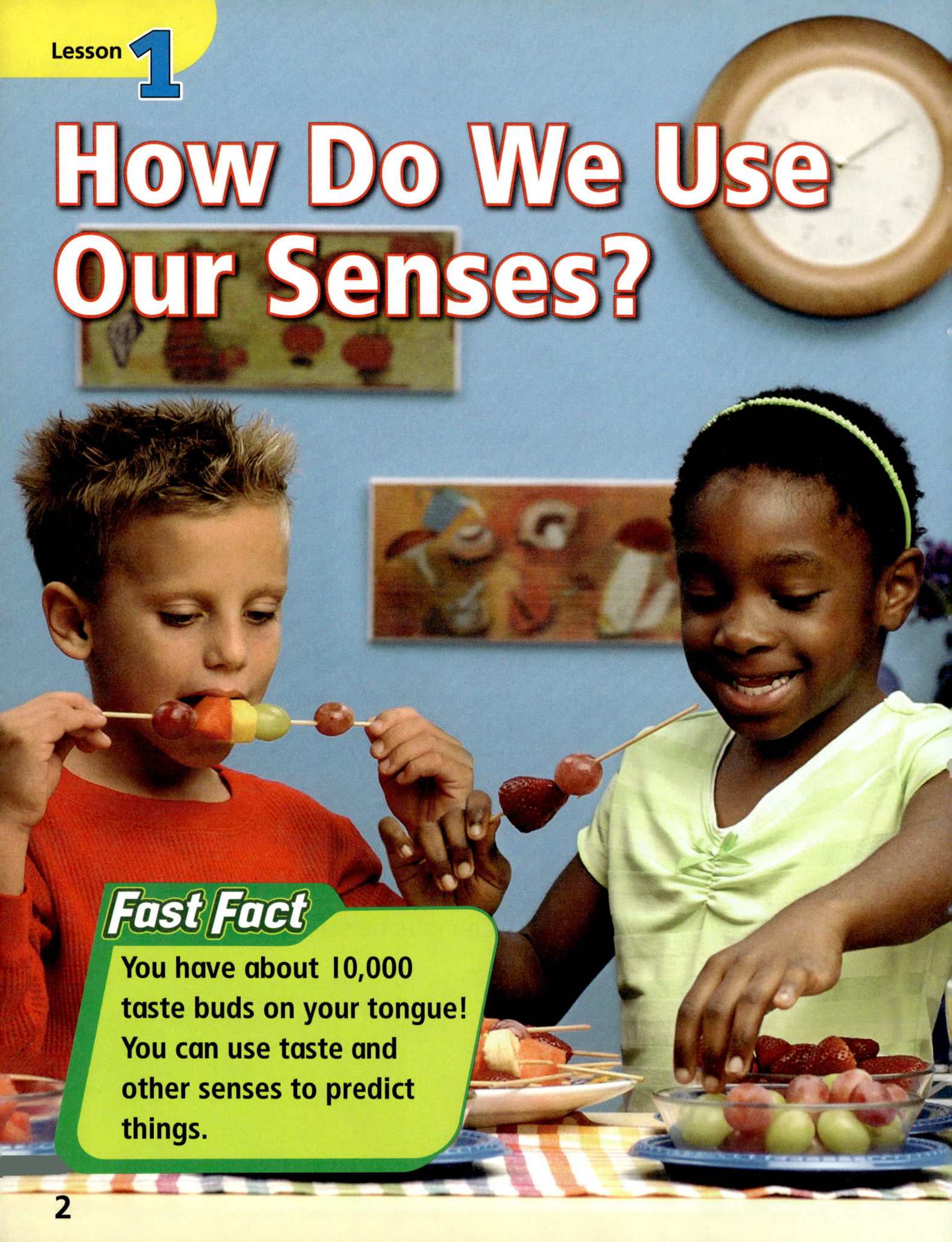

Lesson 1

How Do We Use Our Senses?

Fast Fact

You have about 10,000 taste buds on your tongue! You can use taste and other senses to predict things.

Investigate

How Your Senses Work

You need

- oranges   - bananas   - apples

Step 1

Close your eyes. Your partner will give you a piece of fruit.

Step 2

Smell the fruit. Then taste it. **Predict** which kind of fruit you will see when you open your eyes. Was your **prediction** correct?

Step 3

Trade places with your partner. Repeat.

Inquiry Skill

When you **predict**, you tell what you think will happen.

Reading in Science

VOCABULARY
senses

READING FOCUS SKILL
MAIN IDEA AND DETAILS Look for details about using senses.

Your Senses

People have five senses. The five **senses** are sight, hearing, smell, taste, and touch. You use different body parts for different senses.

MAIN IDEA AND DETAILS
What are the five senses?

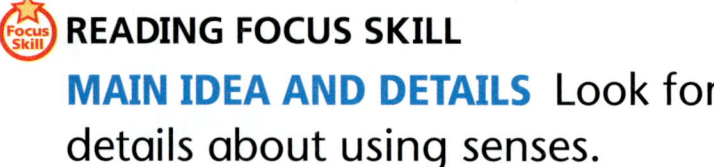

touch
hear
see
smell
taste

Senses Help You

Your senses help you observe and learn about many things.

MAIN IDEA AND DETAILS
How can your senses help you learn?

Insta-Lab

What Do You Hear?
Close your eyes, and listen closely to the sounds around you. Predict what sounds you hear. Open your eyes. Were your predictions correct?

Using Senses Safely

Keep your body safe. Use safety equipment when you need to. Follow these safety rules.

MAIN IDEA AND DETAILS
How can you keep safe?

Wear gloves.
Wear goggles.
Wear an apron.
Don't touch anything hot.
Don't put anything in your mouth unless your teacher tells you to.

Reading Review

1. MAIN IDEA AND DETAILS Copy and complete this chart.

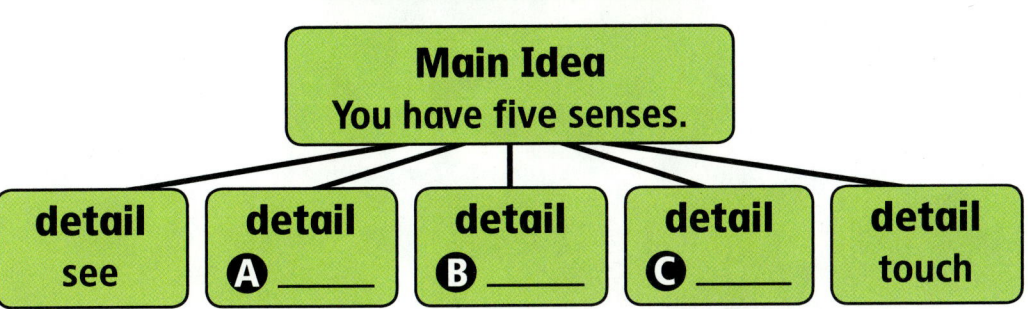

2. SUMMARIZE Use the chart to tell about the lesson.

3. VOCABULARY Use the word **senses** to tell about the picture.

Test Prep
4. Which sense do you use when you feel something?
   A. hearing
   B. smell
   C. taste
   D. touch

Links

Writing

Label Senses
Draw a picture of yourself. What body parts do you use to taste, see, smell, touch, and hear? Label the body parts with the correct sense.

 For more links and activities, go to www.hspscience.com

Lesson 2

How Do We Use Inquiry Skills?

Fast Fact
Pineapples grow on the ground. They have hard, rough peelings. You can draw conclusions about why fruits have peelings.

Investigate

Fruit Protection

You need

• fruits

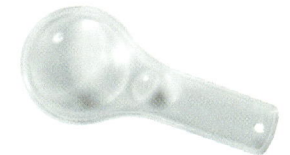
• hand lens

Step 1

Observe some fruits with a hand lens. Look at their peelings.

Step 2

Observe the cut fruits with the hand lens. What is inside the fruit?

Step 3

Draw conclusions about why fruits have peelings.

Inquiry Skill

You **draw conclusions** when you use information to figure out why something is the way it is.

Reading in Science

VOCABULARY
inquiry skills

 READING FOCUS SKILL
MAIN IDEA AND DETAILS Look for details about the inquiry skills scientists use.

Investigating

Scientists follow steps to test things they want to learn about.

1. Observe, and ask a question.

Ask questions. What do you want to know? You can work alone, with a partner, or in a small group.

Is a balloon filled with air heavier than a balloon without air?

2. Form a hypothesis.

Explore your questions. What do you think will happen?

10

3. Plan a fair test.

It is important to be fair. This will help you get correct answers to your questions.

"I'll tie these at the same spot on each end."

4. Do the test.

Try your test. Repeat your test in different places. You should get the same answers.

5. Draw conclusions. Communicate what you learn.

What did you find out? Compare your answers with those of classmates. Share your answers by talking, drawing, or writing.

MAIN IDEA AND DETAILS What steps do scientists follow to test things?

Using Inquiry Skills

Scientists use inquiry skills when they do tests. **Inquiry skills** help people find out information.

communicate

classify

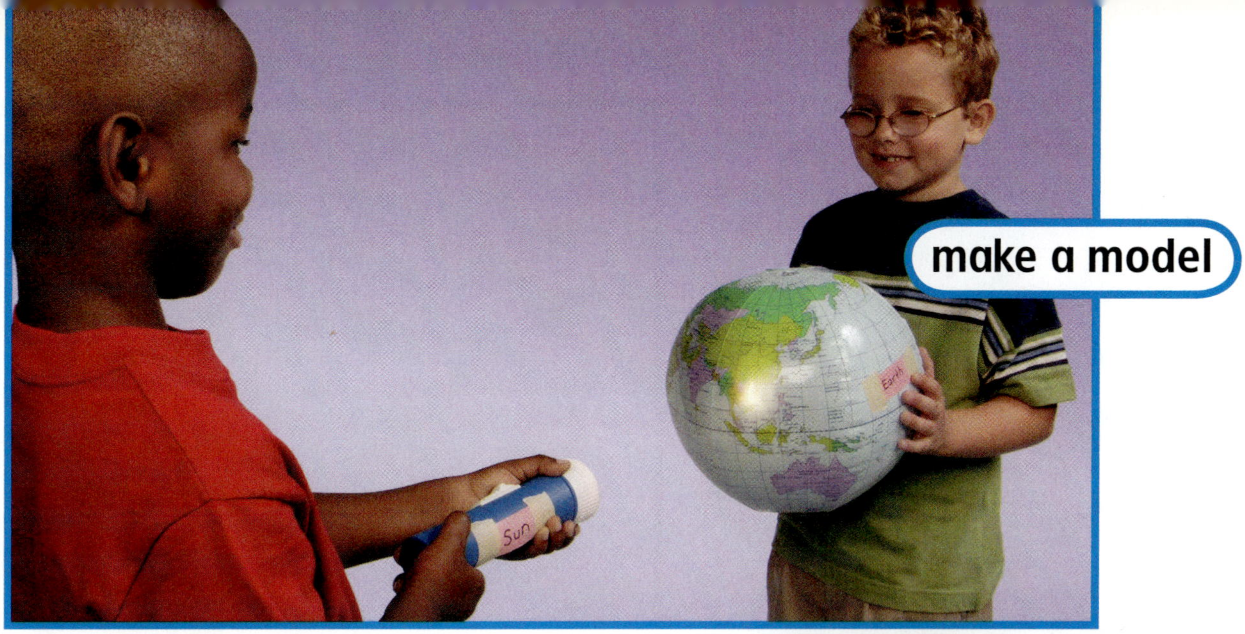
make a model
Sun
Earth

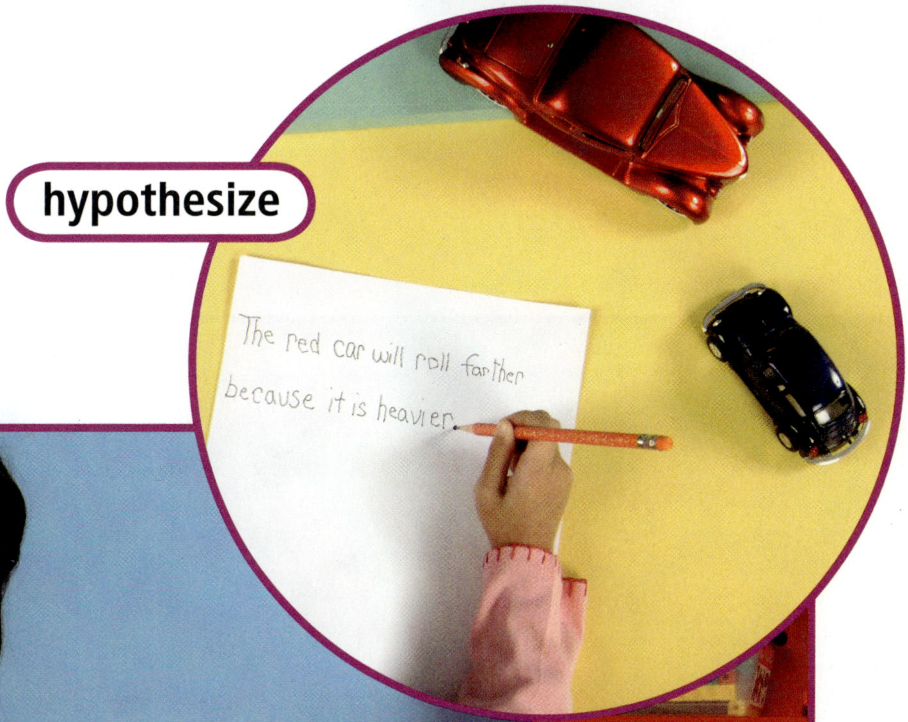
hypothesize
The red car will roll farther
because it is heavier.

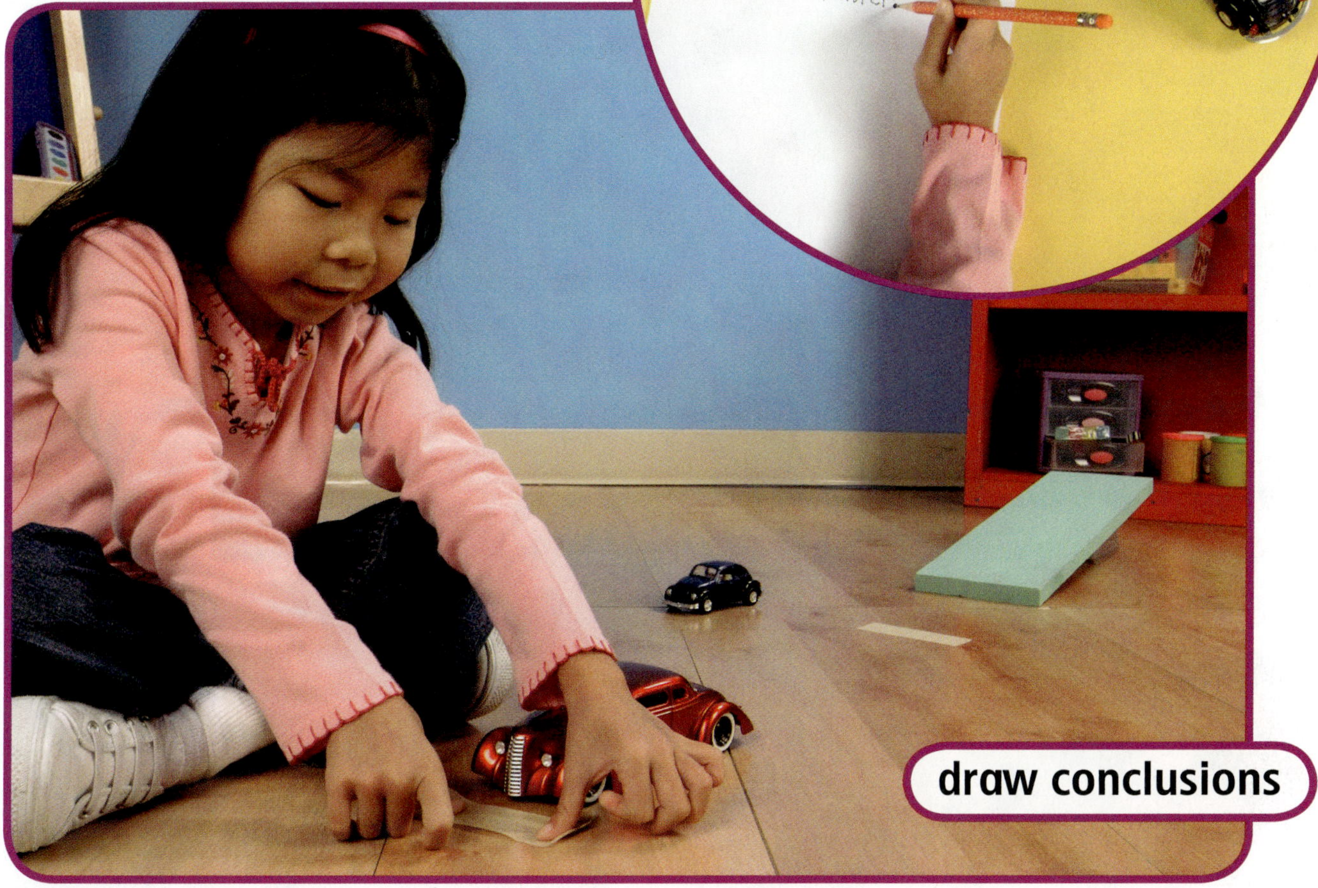
draw conclusions

compare

sequence

measure

observe

predict

plan an investigation

infer

How Far Will It Roll?
Get a ball. Predict how far it will go if you roll it across the floor. Mark that spot with tape. Roll the ball. Was your prediction right?

MAIN IDEA AND DETAILS
What skills do scientists use when they do tests?

16

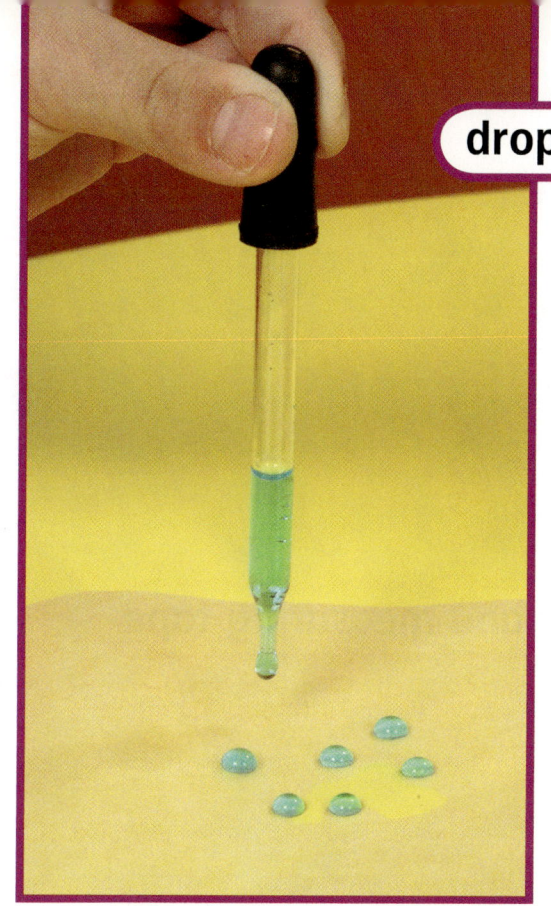

dropper

You can use a dropper to place drops of liquid.

You can use a measuring cup to measure liquid.

measuring cup

thermometer

You can use a thermometer to measure how hot or cold something is.

21

You can use a ruler to measure how long or tall an object is. You can use a measuring tape to measure around an object.

ruler and measuring tape

balance

You can use a balance to measure the mass of an object.

Insta-Lab

Measure It!
Use a tape measure to measure around your arm. Then measure around your leg. Compare the numbers. Which one is greater?

MAIN IDEA AND DETAILS
How can you use science tools to find out information?

Reading Review

1. **MAIN IDEA AND DETAILS** Copy and complete this chart.

   Science Tools

   Main Idea
   You can use science tools.

   detail
   You can use a **A** _____ and a magnifying box to help you see small objects.

   detail
   You can use a balance to measure the **B** _____ of an object.

   detail
   You can use a **C** _____ to measure how hot or cold something is.

2. **DRAW CONCLUSIONS** Draw conclusions about what you can use science tools to do.

3. **VOCABULARY** Use the words **science tools** to tell about the picture.

Test Prep

4. Which would you use to separate things?
   - A. hand lens
   - B. forceps
   - C. ruler
   - D. thermometer

Links

Math

Estimate and Count

Estimate how many cotton balls it will take to fill a measuring cup. Fill the measuring cup with cotton balls. How many did you need? Was the number of cotton balls more or less than you estimated?

 For more links and activities, go to www.hspscience.com

Review and Test Preparation

Vocabulary Review

Use the words to complete the sentences.

senses p. 4
inquiry skills p. 12
science tools p. 20

1. Compare and measure are two ___.

2. Smell is one of your five ___.

3. Scientists use ___ such as droppers and rulers.

Check Understanding

4. Tell **details** about the senses the girl is using in this picture.

5. When you investigate something, what is the next step after you observe and question?

  A. do the test
  B. form a hypothesis
  C. plan the test
  D. draw conclusions and communicate what you learned

Critical Thinking

6. Look at these science tools. Which would you use to make something look larger?

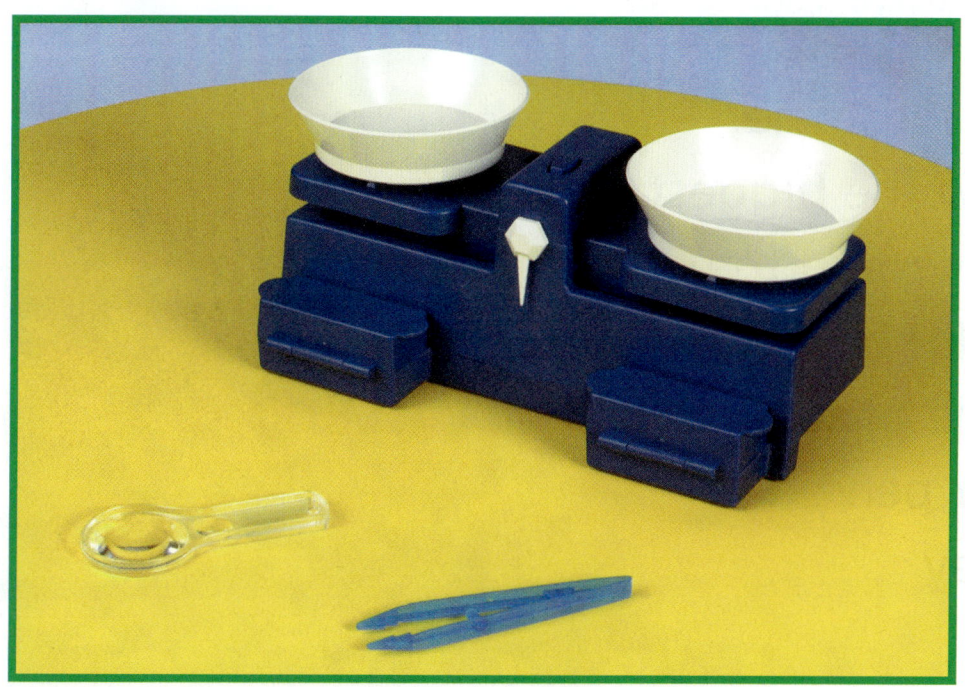

UNIT 1

Animal Diversity

LIFE SCIENCE

| Chapter 1 | All About Animals |
| Chapter 2 | Environments for Living Things |

Sea Lion Caves

TO: jasmine@hspscience.com
FROM: corey@hspscience.com
RE: Oregon Coast

Dear Jasmine,
I saw the biggest sea cave in the world! It is the home of sea lions.
Your pen pal,
Corey

4-H Children's Garden at Michigan State University

TO: vanessa@hspscience.com
FROM: jose@hspscience.com
RE: East Lansing, Michigan

Dear Vanessa,

I went to a garden filled with flowers. The colors of the flowers were just like the colors of our crayons. It was cool!
Jose

Experiment!

Animal Coverings

As you do this unit, you will learn about animals. Plan and do a test. See how animal coverings help them live where they do.

Chapter 1 All About Animals

Lesson 1 What Are Living and Nonliving Things?

Lesson 2 What Do Animals Need?

Lesson 3 How Can We Group Animals?

Lesson 4 How Do Animals Grow and Change?

Vocabulary

living
nonliving
lungs
gills
shelter
mammal
bird
reptile

amphibian
fish
insect
life cycle
tadpole
larva
pupa

Nonliving things do not need food, water, or air. They do not grow. Rocks and water are nonliving things.

COMPARE AND CONTRAST How are all nonliving things alike?

mountain

plants

water

Insta-Lab

Compare Living Things
Look at a living thing. Draw what you see. Then compare your picture with a partner's picture. Are both things living? Talk about how you know.

Classify Living and Nonliving Things

You can classify things as living or nonliving. Living things need food, water, and air. They grow and change. If something is not like living things in these two ways, then it is nonliving.

⭐ **COMPARE AND CONTRAST** Look at the chart. How are the living things different from the nonliving things?

Reading Review

1. **MAIN IDEA AND DETAILS** Copy and complete this chart.

```
            Animal Needs
    ┌────────┬────────┬────────┐
   food    water    air     shelter
```

- **food**: Animals need food to live.
- **water**: Some get water by drinking. Some get it from the **A** _____ they eat.
- **air**: Some get air with **B** _____. Some get it with gills.
- **shelter**: Shelter is a place to be **C** _____.

2. **DRAW CONCLUSIONS** What are four things that animals need?

3. **VOCABULARY** Use the word **shelter** to talk about this picture.

Test Prep

4. What do animals use gills and lungs for?
   A. to move
   B. to get water
   C. to get air
   D. to get shelter

Links

Math

Counting Breaths

Count your breaths for one minute after resting. Count your breaths again after running. When did you take more breaths? How many more?

 For more links and activities, go to www.hspscience.com

Lesson 3

How Can We Group Animals?

Fast Fact

Feathers help birds fly. They also help keep birds warm. Looking at body coverings can help you classify animals.

Investigate

Classify Animals

You need

- crayons

- paper

Step 1

Observe different kinds of animals.

Step 2

Draw pictures to record your observations.

Step 3

Classify the animals into groups. Tell how you **classified** the animals in each group.

Inquiry Skill

Classify animals to help you see how they are alike and different.

43

Reading in Science

VOCABULARY
mammal   amphibian
bird   fish
reptile insect

 READING FOCUS SKILL

MAIN IDEA AND DETAILS Look for the main idea and details about each kind of animal.

Mammals

A **mammal** is an animal that has hair or fur. Almost all mammals give birth to live young. The young drink milk from their mother's body.

seal and pup

MAIN IDEA AND DETAILS
What is a mammal?

tiger

bird feeding chicks

Birds

A **bird** is the only kind of animal that has feathers. Most birds use their wings to fly. Birds have their young by laying eggs. They find food to feed their young.

 MAIN IDEA AND DETAILS
How can you tell if an animal is a bird?

peacock

Reptiles and Amphibians

A **reptile** has scaly, dry skin. Lizards and turtles are reptiles.

gecko

turtle

Most **amphibians** have smooth, wet skin. Young amphibians hatch from eggs that are laid in the water. As adults, they live on land. Frogs are amphibians.

frog

MAIN IDEA AND DETAILS
What kind of animal has smooth, wet skin?

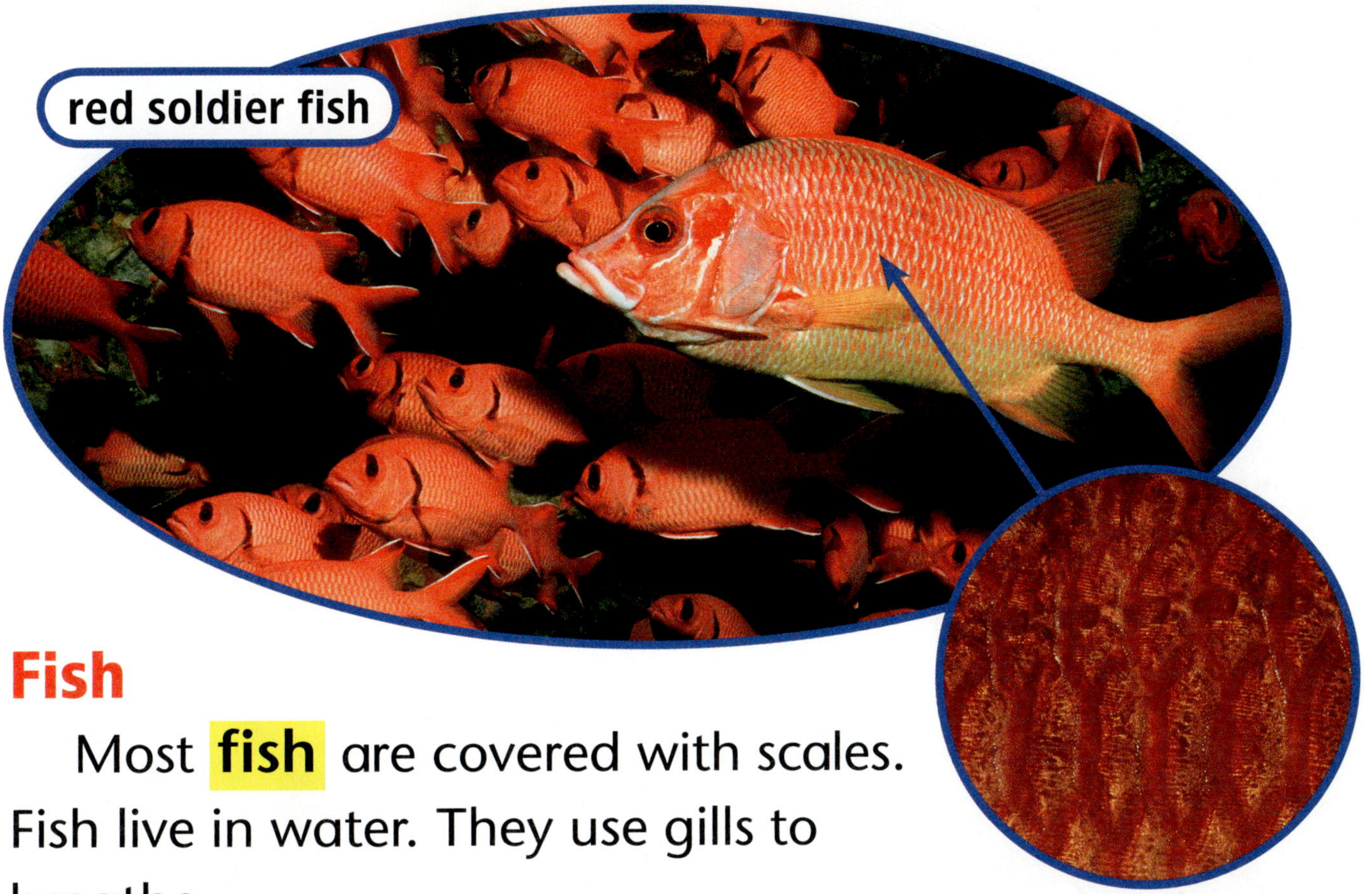

red soldier fish

Fish

Most **fish** are covered with scales. Fish live in water. They use gills to breathe.

MAIN IDEA AND DETAILS
How do fish breathe?

sailfish

47

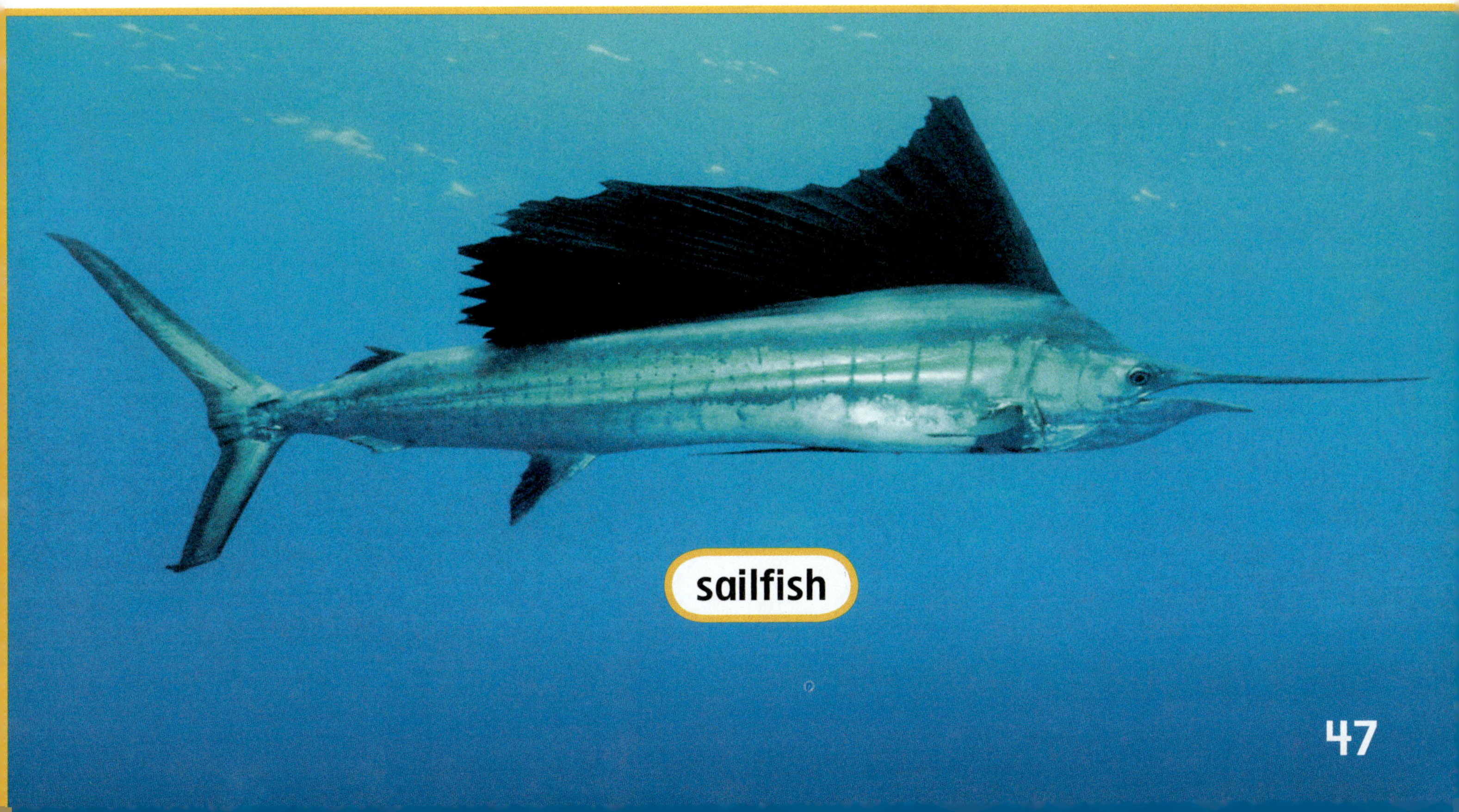

Insects

An **insect** is an animal that has three body parts and six legs. Insects do not have bones. A hard shell keeps their soft insides safe.

 MAIN IDEA AND DETAILS How many parts does an insect's body have?

beetle

ants

Many Legs Chart
Count the legs of animals in this lesson. Use the data to make a chart. Then use your chart to compare numbers of legs.

butterfly

48

Reading Review

1. **MAIN IDEA AND DETAILS** Copy and complete this chart.

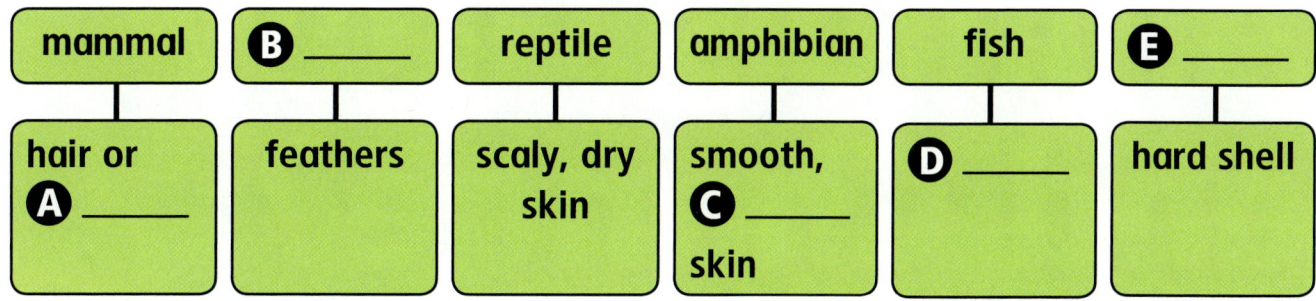

2. **DRAW CONCLUSIONS** Which two animal groups do you think are the most alike? Explain.

3. **VOCABULARY** Use the word **bird** to tell about this animal.

Test Prep

4. What kind of animal feeds its young with milk from its body?
   A. a bird
   B. a fish
   C. an insect
   D. a mammal

Links

Art

Patterned Wrapping Paper
Make animal-pattern wrapping paper. Look at patterns on butterfly wings and on other animals. Choose a pattern you like. Copy it onto a large piece of paper. Color it with crayons or paint.

 For more links and activities, go to www.hspscience.com

Lesson 4

How Do Animals Grow and Change?

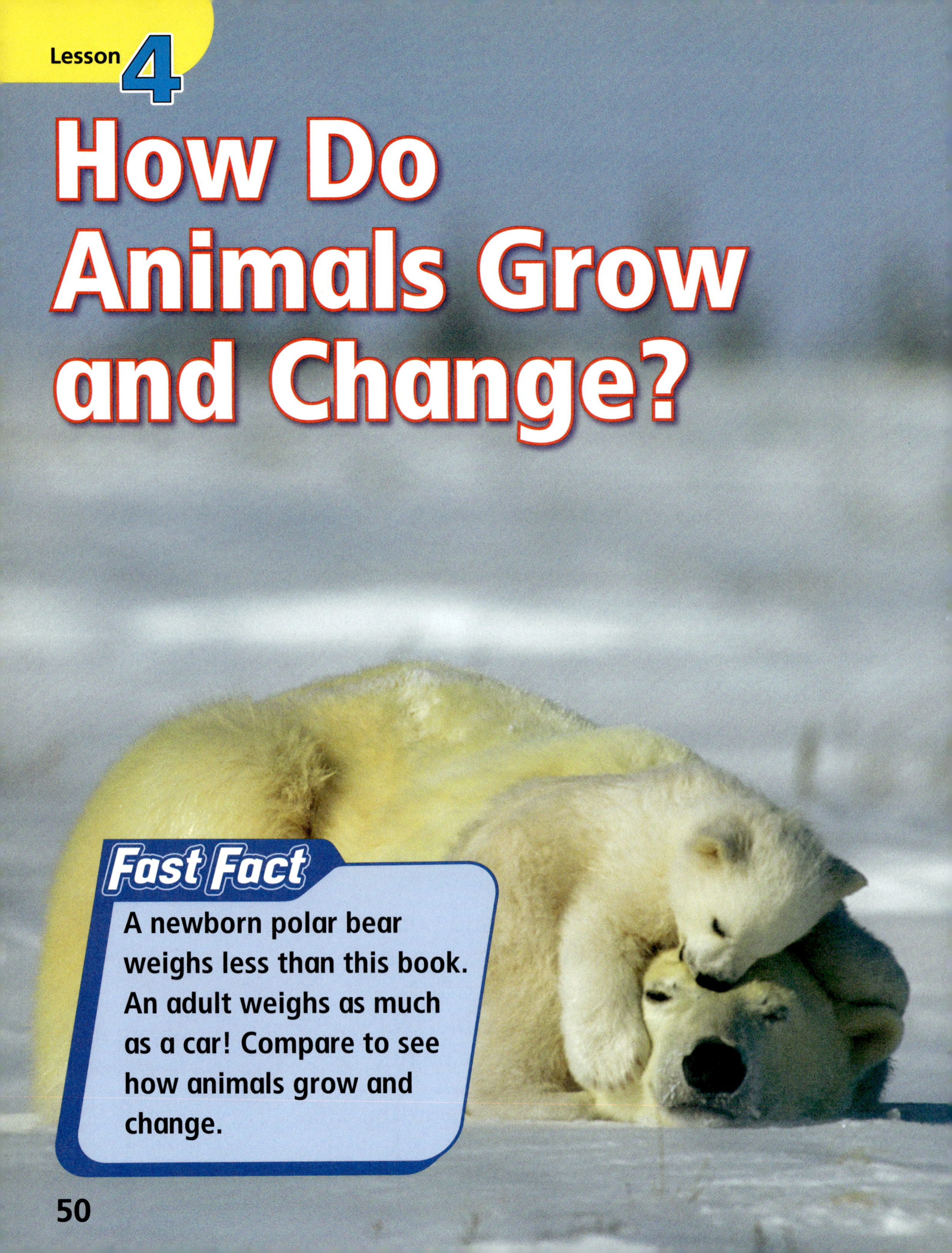

Fast Fact

A newborn polar bear weighs less than this book. An adult weighs as much as a car! Compare to see how animals grow and change.

Investigate

Animals Grow and Change

You need

- animal picture cards

Step 1

Look at the picture cards. Match each adult animal with its young.

Step 2

Make a chart to **compare** adult animals with their young.

Animals and Their Young		
Animal	Same	Different
sea turtles	Both have flippers.	One is big. One is small.

Step 3

Write about how each adult animal is like its young and how it is different.

Inquiry Skill

Compare adult animals and their young. How are they alike and different?

51

Reading in Science

VOCABULARY
life cycle
tadpole
larva
pupa

 READING FOCUS SKILL

SEQUENCE Look for ways each animal changes as it grows.

How a Frog Grows

A **life cycle** is all of the parts of an animal's life.

A frog's life cycle starts as an egg in water. A **tadpole**, or young frog, comes out of the egg. Its tail helps it swim. It breathes with gills.

eggs

about 7 weeks

about 2 weeks

52

The tadpole grows legs, and its tail gets smaller. It starts to use lungs to breathe. Soon it is an adult frog. It lives on land most of the time.

SEQUENCE How does a tadpole change as it grows?

about 14 weeks

about 9 weeks

How a Butterfly Grows

A butterfly also starts its life cycle as an egg. A **larva**, or caterpillar, comes out of the egg. The larva eats and grows.

The larva stops eating. It becomes a **pupa** with a hard covering. Inside, the pupa changes into a butterfly. At last, an adult butterfly comes out.

SEQUENCE What happens after the larva stops eating?

egg

larva

adult butterfly

butterfly comes out

pupa

Insta-Lab

Be a Butterfly

Act out a butterfly's life cycle. What happens first, next, and last? How can you move your body to show what happens?

Science Up Close

Animals and Their Young

Dogs are mammals. The puppies look like their parents, but they are not just like them. They are not just like each other. Each puppy is a little different.

How does a puppy change as it grows?

How is it like its parents?

just-born puppies

about 2 months old

adult dog

For more links and activities, go to www.hspscience.com

Reading Review

 1. SEQUENCE Copy and complete this chart.

Life Cycle of A Butterfly

A butterfly lays an **A** _____.

A **B** _____ comes out. It eats and grows.

A **C** _____ has a hard covering.

An adult comes out.

2. SUMMARIZE Write sentences that tell what this lesson is about.

3. VOCABULARY Use the word **tadpole** to talk about this picture.

Test Prep

4. Which animal is a larva and a pupa for parts of its life cycle?
- **A.** butterfly
- **B.** cat
- **C.** dog
- **D.** frog

Links

Math

Compare Animal Young

This chart shows the number of young some animals may have at one time. Use the data to make a bar graph.

Animal Young	
elephant	1
cat	5
owl	6
cockroach	30
crocodile	60

 For more links and activities, go to www.hspscience.com

57

Traveling Turtles:
A Trip Across the Atlantic

In late spring, huge sea turtles crawl onto a beach in Florida. Each turtle digs a nest in the sand. The mother turtle then lays about 100 eggs. Two months later, tiny turtles hatch.

The young turtles crawl out of their holes and into the ocean.

A Long Trip

The tiny turtles set out on a long trip. They swim across the Atlantic Ocean and back again. The trip takes between five and ten years. The trip is thousands of miles long.

Scientists wanted to know how the turtles made their way across the ocean. To find out, scientists put "bathing suits" on some young sea turtles. The bathing suits were tied to special machines. The special machines can follow how the turtles swim.

THINK ABOUT IT

How long will it take for a young turtle to swim across the Atlantic Ocean?

Find out more! Log on to www.hspscience.com

Feeding Time

Chloe Ruiz went to the petting zoo with her family. Chloe saw pigs, horses, and cows.

The people at the zoo asked Chloe if she wanted to help feed a young cow. A young cow is called a calf.

Chloe fed the calf milk. She used a bottle to feed the calf. She knows the calf needs to drink lots of milk to help it grow.

SCIENCE Projects
for Home or School
You Can Do It!

Which Foods Birds Like

What to Do
1. Put bread crumbs in one pie plate. Put fruit in the other.
2. Put both plates on a table outside.
3. Observe the birds that eat from each plate. Draw pictures to record your observations.

Materials
- 2 foil pie plates
- bread crumbs
- chopped apples and grapes

Draw Conclusions
Do different birds eat different foods? How do you know?

Animals and Their Young

Mammals and birds care for their young. Choose one. Find out how it helps its young. Make models to show how the animal cares for its young.

Chapter 1 Review and Test Preparation

Vocabulary Review

Tell which picture goes best with each word.

1. mammal p. 44
2. bird p. 45
3. fish p. 47
4. insect p. 48

A.  B.  C.  D.

Check Understanding

5. Show the **sequence**. Write **first**, **next**, **then**, and **last**.

A.  B.  C.  D.

6. Which is **true** about frogs?

   A. They are fish.

   B. They have scaly, dry skin.

   C. The young are called tadpoles.

   D. Adults breathe with gills.

Critical Thinking

7. Compare the pigs. Which one is living? Which is not? Tell how you know.

8. Think about a pet you want. Draw a picture of the pet. List each thing it needs. Tell how you would help it meet its needs.

Chapter

2 Environments for Living Things

Lesson 1 What Is an Environment?

Lesson 2 What Helps Plants and Animals Live in Places?

Lesson 3 How Do Plants and Animals Need Each Other?

Vocabulary
environment
adaptation
camouflage
oxygen
pollen
food chain

Reading in Science

VOCABULARY
environment

 **READING FOCUS SKILL**

MAIN IDEA AND DETAILS Look for the main ideas about environments.

Environments

An **environment** is made up of all the things in a place.

An environment has living things. It has plants and animals.

Find living and nonliving things in this environment.

Investigate

Where Animals Live

You need

- animal picture cards
- crayons

Step 1

Look at the cards. Choose an animal you know about.

Step 2

Draw the animal where it lives.

Step 3

Communicate with classmates about what you drew.

Inquiry Skill

When you **communicate**, you tell about each thing you drew in your picture.

Lesson 1

What Is an Environment?

Fast Fact

Few people have ever seen jaguars in the wild. They live where it is easy to hide. Communicate what you know about where animals live.

I wonder...

Why do these insects look like plants?

What do you wonder?

65

An environment also has nonliving things, such as rocks and water.

MAIN IDEA AND DETAILS
What is an environment?

Insta-Lab

Environments Near You

Go on a nature walk with your class. Observe the environment. What living things do you see? What nonliving things do you see? Make two lists.

69

People and Environments

People can change environments. They may build houses and roads. They may make new things. People made many of the things you see in your environment.

> **MAIN IDEA AND DETAILS** How can people change environments?

Which things here did people make? Which things were not made by people?

Reading Review

1. **MAIN IDEA AND DETAILS** Copy and complete this chart.

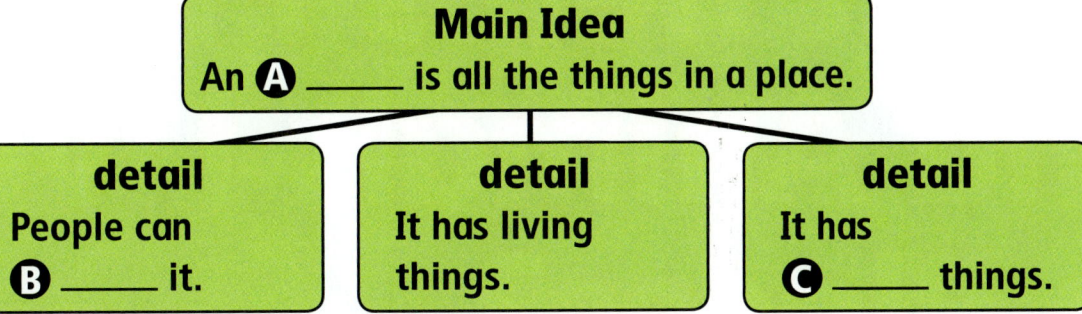

2. **SUMMARIZE** Use the chart to write a lesson summary.

3. **VOCABULARY** Tell about this animal's **environment**.

Test Prep

4. Tell about some ways people can change their environments.

Links

Writing

Write a Description

Look at the environment outside your school. Write sentences about things you see that were made by people. Tell what each thing looks like. Tell what it is used for.

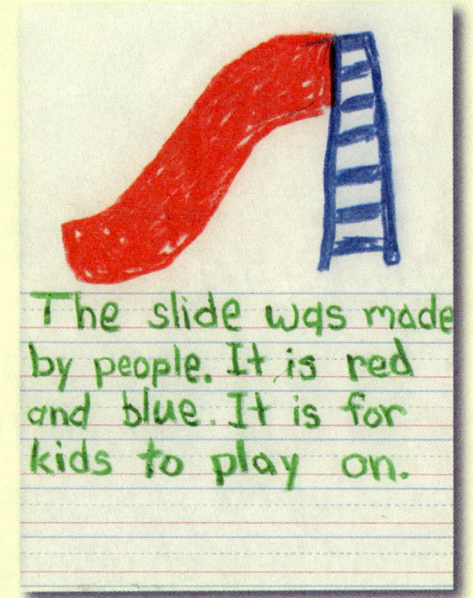

 For more links and activities, go to www.hspscience.com

71

Lesson 2

What Helps Plants and Animals Live in Places?

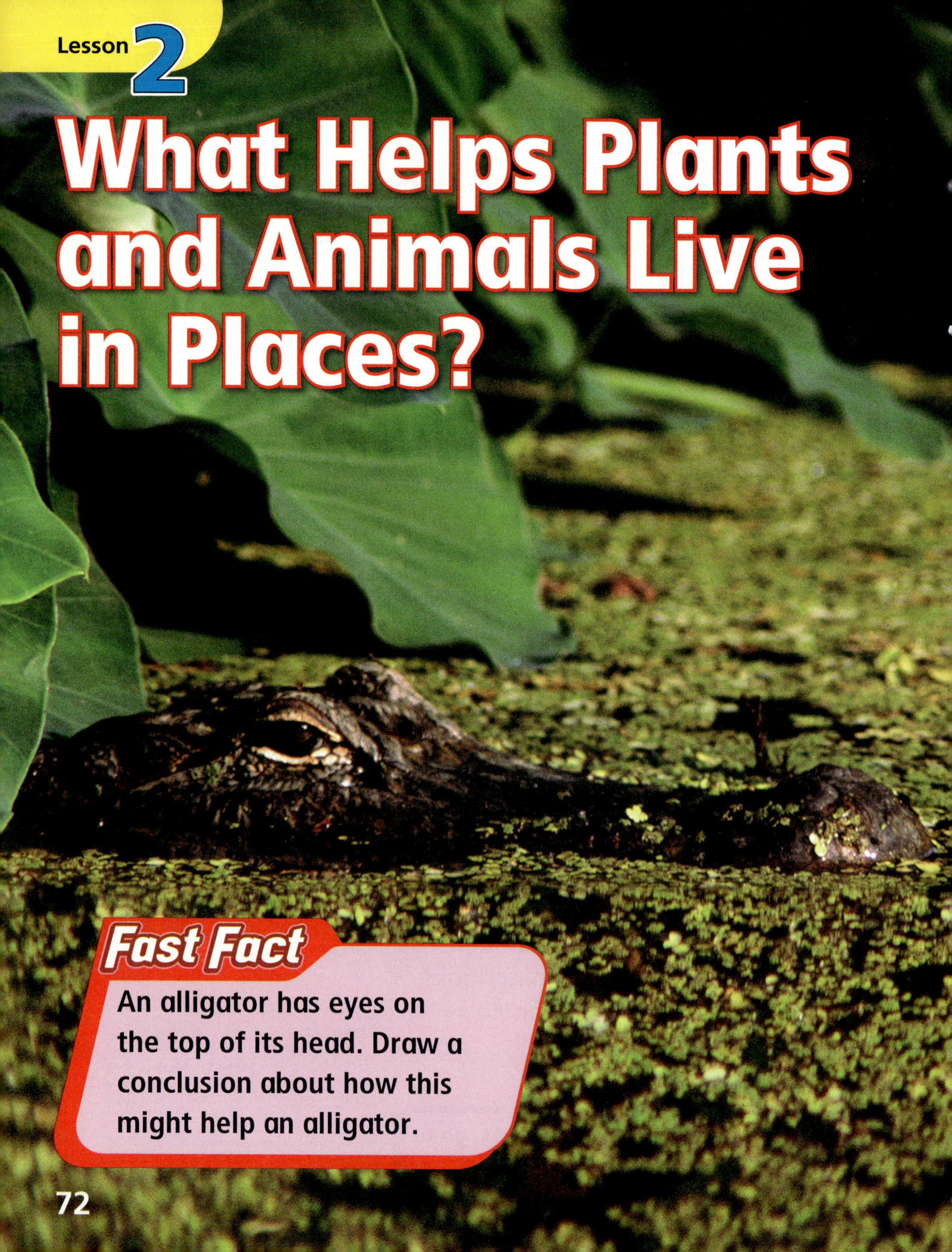

Fast Fact
An alligator has eyes on the top of its head. Draw a conclusion about how this might help an alligator.

Investigate

Some Animals Hide

You need

- colored paper clips

- colored paper

Step 1

Put the clips on a sheet of colored paper. Which clips are hard to see?

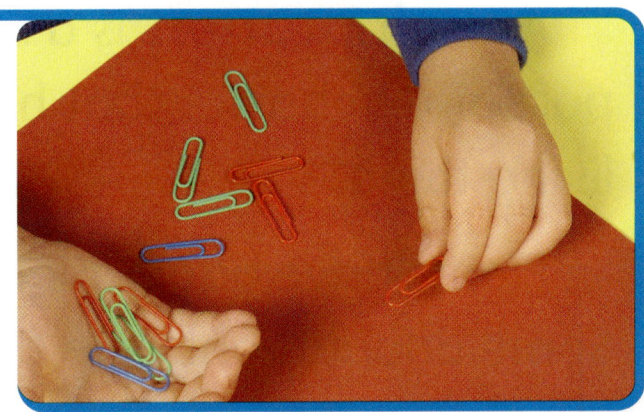

Step 2

Put the clips on a sheet of paper of a different color. Which clips are hard to see now?

Step 3

Draw a conclusion about how color helps some animals hide.

Inquiry Skill

To **draw a conclusion** about animals' colors, think about the clips that were hard to see.

Reading in Science

VOCABULARY
adaptation
camouflage

 READING FOCUS SKILL

COMPARE AND CONTRAST Look for ways adaptations are alike and different.

Plant Adaptations

An **adaptation** is a body part or a behavior that helps a living thing.

Plants have adaptations. Some adaptations help them get water. A banyan tree has many roots. A jade plant has thick leaves that store water.

banyan tree

jade plant

Some adaptations help plants stay alive. Thorns on plants stop animals from eating them. Other adaptations help plants make new plants. Wings on maple seeds carry the seeds to new places. Flowers attract small animals. The animals help the plants make seeds.

maple seeds

⭐ **COMPARE AND CONTRAST** What are some plant adaptations? How are they alike and different?

hummingbird

rose

Animal Adaptations

Animals have adaptations, too. Some adaptations help animals eat. Sharp teeth help a lion bite meat. A long tongue helps an anteater get ants.

Some adaptations help animals move. Wings and feathers help a bird fly. Fins help a fish swim.

scarlet ibis

lion

anteater

Reading Review

 1. COMPARE AND CONTRAST Copy and complete this chart.

Adaptation

alike
- A _____ help living things.

different
- Some help plants get B _____.
- Some help plants stay alive or C _____.
- Some help animals D _____.
- Some help E _____ move.
- Some help animals stay F _____.

2. DRAW CONCLUSIONS Why do you think some animals have camouflage?

3. VOCABULARY Use the word **adaptation** to tell about this picture.

Test Prep

4. Which adaptation helps plants store water?
- A. flowers
- B. sharp teeth
- C. thick leaves
- D. thorns

Links

Math

Counting Teeth

Some animals have many teeth. Others do not. How many teeth do you have? Use a mirror to count. Use the data to make a class graph. Does everyone have the same number of teeth?

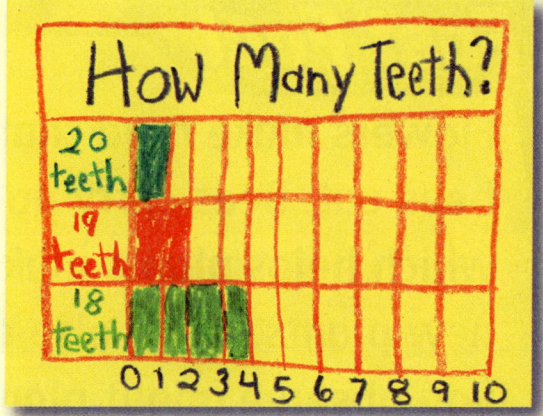

 For more links and activities, go to www.hspscience.com

Lesson 3

How Do Plants and Animals Need Each Other?

Fast Fact

Flowers make food that bees eat. Bees carry pollen, which helps plants make new plants. What else can you observe about plants and animals?

Investigate

Animals in a Tree

You need

- hand lens

Step 1

Find a tree with your class. **Observe** it with a hand lens. Record what you see.

Step 2

Sit quietly and **observe**. Record what animals in your tree are doing.

Step 3

How did animals use the tree? Talk about what you **observed**.

Inquiry Skill

Use your senses to help you **observe**.

Reading in Science

VOCABULARY
oxygen
pollen
food chain

 READING FOCUS SKILL

MAIN IDEA AND DETAILS Look for the main ideas about how animals use plants and help plants.

Animals Use Plants

Animals use plants to meet their needs. Some live in plants or use them to make homes. Plants are good places for animals to hide in, too.

heron hiding in grass

deer hiding behind trees

beaver building a dam

Some animals use plants for food. Animals need to breathe oxygen from the air. **Oxygen** is a kind of gas. Plants put oxygen into the air.

★ **MAIN IDEA AND DETAILS**
What are three ways animals use plants?

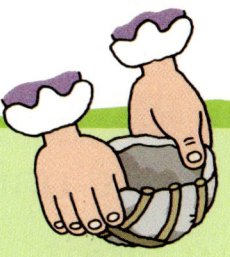

Homes from Plants
Some birds use plant parts and mud to make nests. Use twigs, grass, and clay to make a model of a bird's nest.

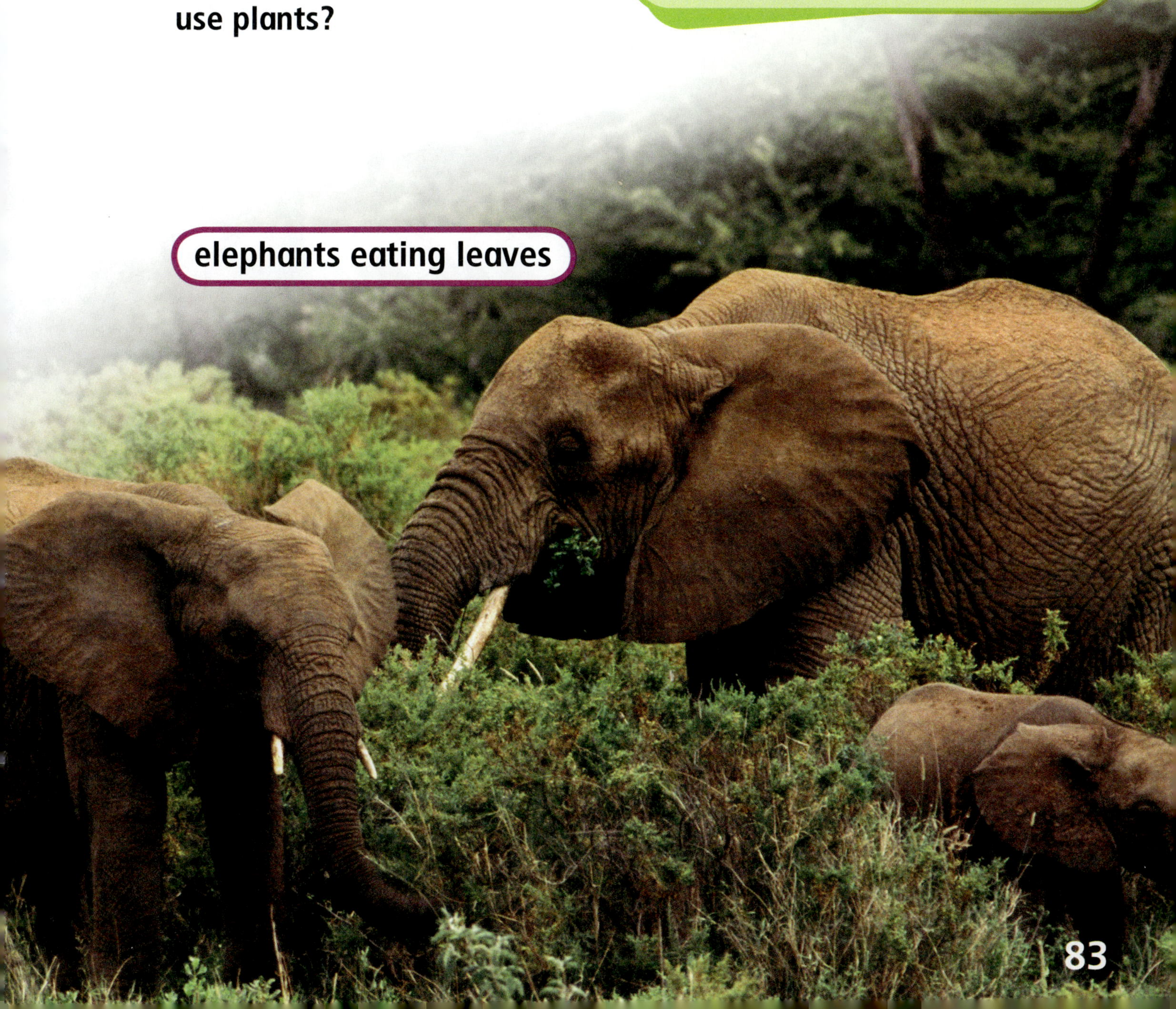

elephants eating leaves

83

Animals Help Plants

Some animals help plants make new plants. They carry **pollen** from flower to flower. Pollen is a powder that flowers need to make seeds.

honey possum carrying pollen

butterfly carrying pollen

Some animals help plants by carrying seeds. They take seeds to new places. The seeds may grow into new plants there.

★ **MAIN IDEA AND DETAILS**
How can animals help plants make new plants?

squirrel carrying seeds

dog carrying seeds

Food Chain

Animals can be grouped by what they eat. Some animals eat plants. Some eat other animals. A **food chain** shows how animals and plants are linked.

MAIN IDEA AND DETAILS
What does a food chain show?

Last, a bear eats the fish.

Next, a rainbow trout eats the stonefly.

First, a stonefly eats part of a plant.

Reading Review

 1. **MAIN IDEA AND DETAILS** Copy and complete this chart.

Main Idea
Animals and plants need each other.

- **detail** Animals eat **A** _____.
- **detail** Animals carry **B** _____ from flower to flower.
- **detail** Animals use plants for **C** _____.
- **detail** Animals carry **D** _____ to new places.

2. **SUMMARIZE** Write two sentences to summarize the lesson.

3. **VOCABULARY** Use the word **pollen** to tell about this animal.

Test Prep

4. Which of these shows how animals are linked?
   - A. air
   - B. environment
   - C. flowers
   - D. food chain

Links

 **Social Studies**

You Need Plants and Animals

How do you use plants and animals to meet your needs? Draw pictures and write sentences to show the ways. Put your pages together to make a book.

For more links and activities, go to www.hspscience.com

87

SCIENCE Spin from WEEKLY READER

Technology

Now You See It, Now You Don't

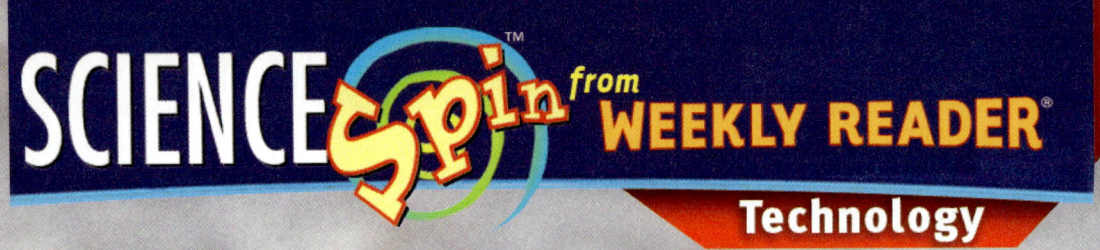

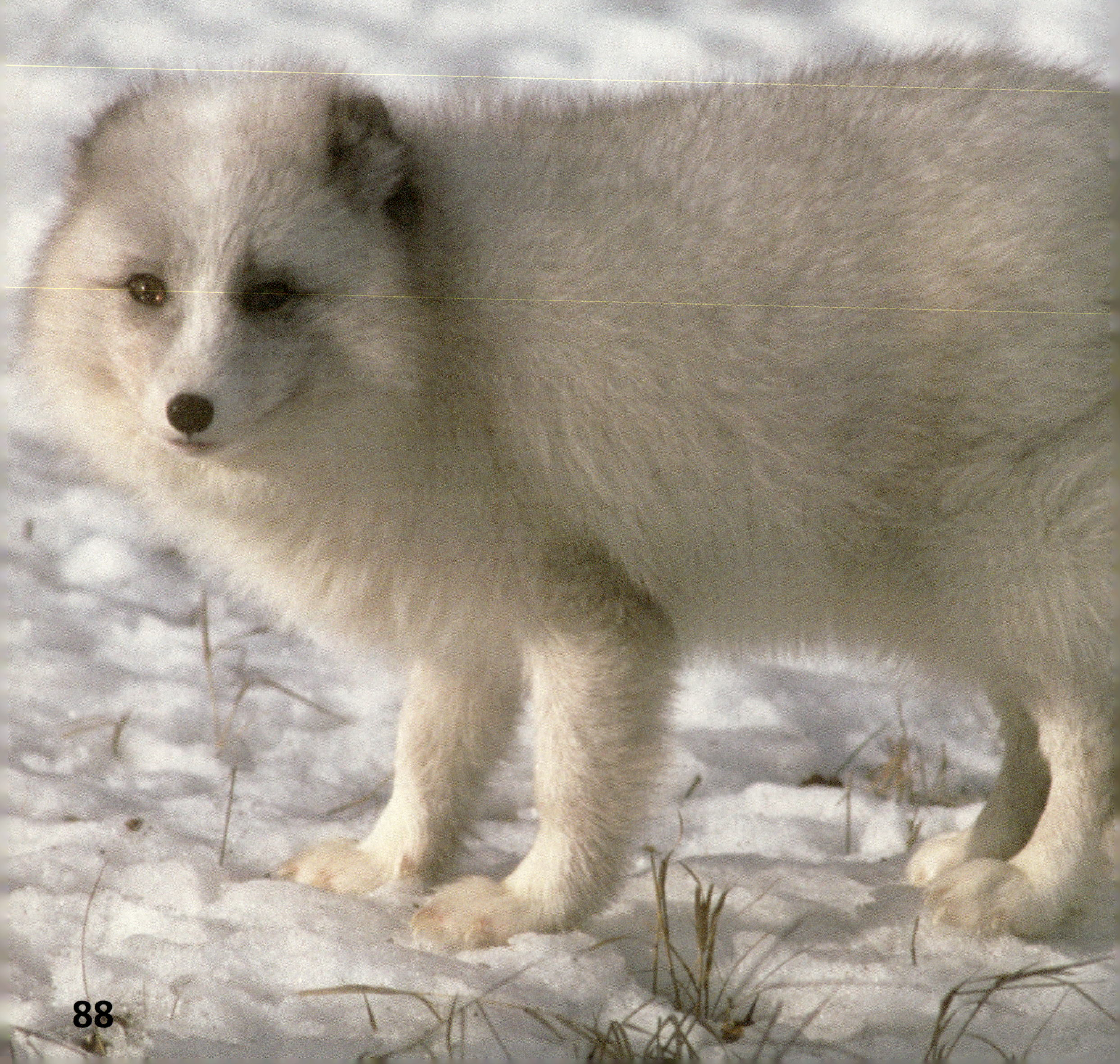

Do you ever wish you could hide like an artic fox? Now your wish can come true.

Susumu Tachi is a teacher. He lives in Japan. Tachi made a coat to show how things can be hidden.

Tiny Glass Beads

The coat is covered by many tiny glass beads. The beads reflect light. Then you can see through a person wearing the coat.

THINK ABOUT IT
How is this coat similar to camouflage?

Seeing into the Future

Tachi says his idea might be used in many ways. Doctors could use tools with the beads on them. Then they could see through the tools when they operate.

Find out more! Log on to www.hspscience.com

Where Are All the Butterflies?

People often see monarch butterflies in the fall. The insects leave places in the north when the weather turns cold. They fly to warmer places in the south. Scientists want to know why.

Emma Griffiths helped scientists count butterflies. Emma helped by scooping up butterflies. Then scientists put a tiny tag on each insect. The tag shows other scientists that the butterflies came from Connecticut.

SCIENCE Projects for Home or School
You Can Do It!

What Makes Seeds Stick?

Materials
- foam ball
- glue
- rough materials

What to Do
1. Find some seeds. Which ones might stick to animals?
2. Make a model of a seed that will stick to things.
3. Does your model stick to your clothes? How does this help you understand how seeds stick to animals?

Draw Conclusions
How is the ball a model of a seed that sticks to things?

Watch a Plant Change

Put two plants that are the same by a window. Mark one. Each day, turn the other plant. Do not turn the marked plant. After one week, how has the marked plant changed? Why did it do this?

Chapter 2

Review and Test Preparation

Vocabulary Review

Choose the best word to complete each sentence.

environment p. 68   **oxygen** p. 83
camouflage p. 78   **pollen** p. 84

1. Powder from flowers is ___.

2. A gas that is part of air is ___.

3. An adaptation that helps an animal hide is ___.

4. A place that is made up of living and nonliving things is an ___.

Check Understanding

5. Name two animals. Tell how the adaptations of these animals are **alike**. Then tell how they are **different**.

6. How do plants help animals breathe?

    A. Plants put oxygen into the air.

    B. Animals eat plants.

    C. Plants store water.

    D. Animals can hide in plants.

Critical Thinking

7. Why do you think people change their environments? How do some changes harm the plants and animals that live there?

8. Look at these plants and animals. Draw them in order to show a food chain. Write about what happens.

UNIT 2
Properties of Matter

| Chapter 3 | All About Matter |
| Chapter 4 | Heat, Light, and Sound |

PHYSICAL SCIENCE

Albuquerque International Balloon Fiesta

TO: carmen@hspscience.com
FROM: louisa@hspscience.com
RE: Albuquerque, New Mexico

Dear Carmen,
Marta and I went to a festival. Lots of colored balloons floated in the sky. People took rides in the baskets. I got to ride in one too!
Louisa

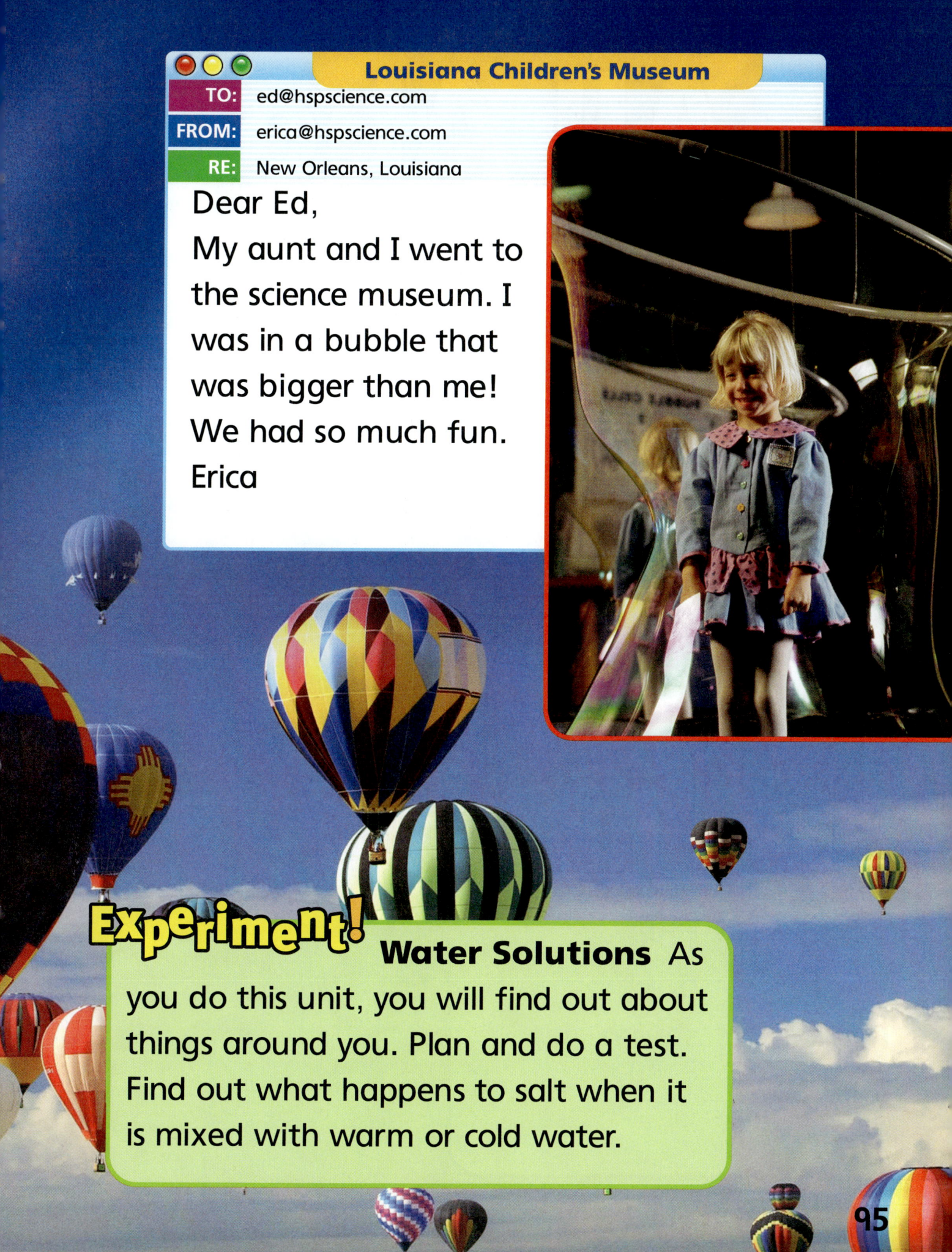

Louisiana Children's Museum

TO: ed@hspscience.com
FROM: erica@hspscience.com
RE: New Orleans, Louisiana

Dear Ed,
My aunt and I went to the science museum. I was in a bubble that was bigger than me! We had so much fun.
Erica

Experiment!

Water Solutions As you do this unit, you will find out about things around you. Plan and do a test. Find out what happens to salt when it is mixed with warm or cold water.

Chapter 3 All About Matter

Lesson 1 **What Is Matter?**

Lesson 2 **What Can We Observe About Solids?**

Lesson 3 **What Can We Observe About Liquids?**

Lesson 4 **What Can We Observe About Gases?**

Vocabulary

matter
solid
mixture
length
mass
liquid
dissolve
float
sink
gas
steam

I wonder...

Why do things filled with air float in water?

What do you wonder?

Lesson 1

What Is Matter?

Fast Fact

The largest stuffed bear was 32 feet tall. You can classify toys by size, shape, and color.

Investigate

Classify Matter

You need

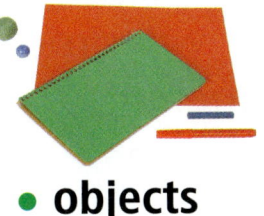

- objects

Step 1

Observe the objects. Compare their sizes, shapes, and colors.

Step 2

Classify the objects in three ways.

Step 3

Draw pictures of the groups you made.

Inquiry Skill

When you **classify** objects, you sort them by how they are alike.

Reading in Science

VOCABULARY
matter

 READING FOCUS SKILL

COMPARE AND CONTRAST Look for ways matter can be alike and different.

Matter

Everything around you is **matter**. Toys are matter. Balloons are matter. Water is matter, too. Some matter has parts that are too hard to see.

What matter do you see here?

100

All matter is not the same. Matter can be soft or hard. It can be big or small.

⭐ **COMPARE AND CONTRAST** How are the stuffed toy and balloons alike? How are they different?

Insta-Lab

Matter Up Close

Observe sand and soil with a hand lens. How are they alike? How are they different? What does the hand lens help you see? Talk to a partner about what you see.

101

Sorting Matter

You can sort matter. You can sort these objects by color. You can sort them by shape. How else can you sort them?

COMPARE AND CONTRAST How could you sort these objects by color?

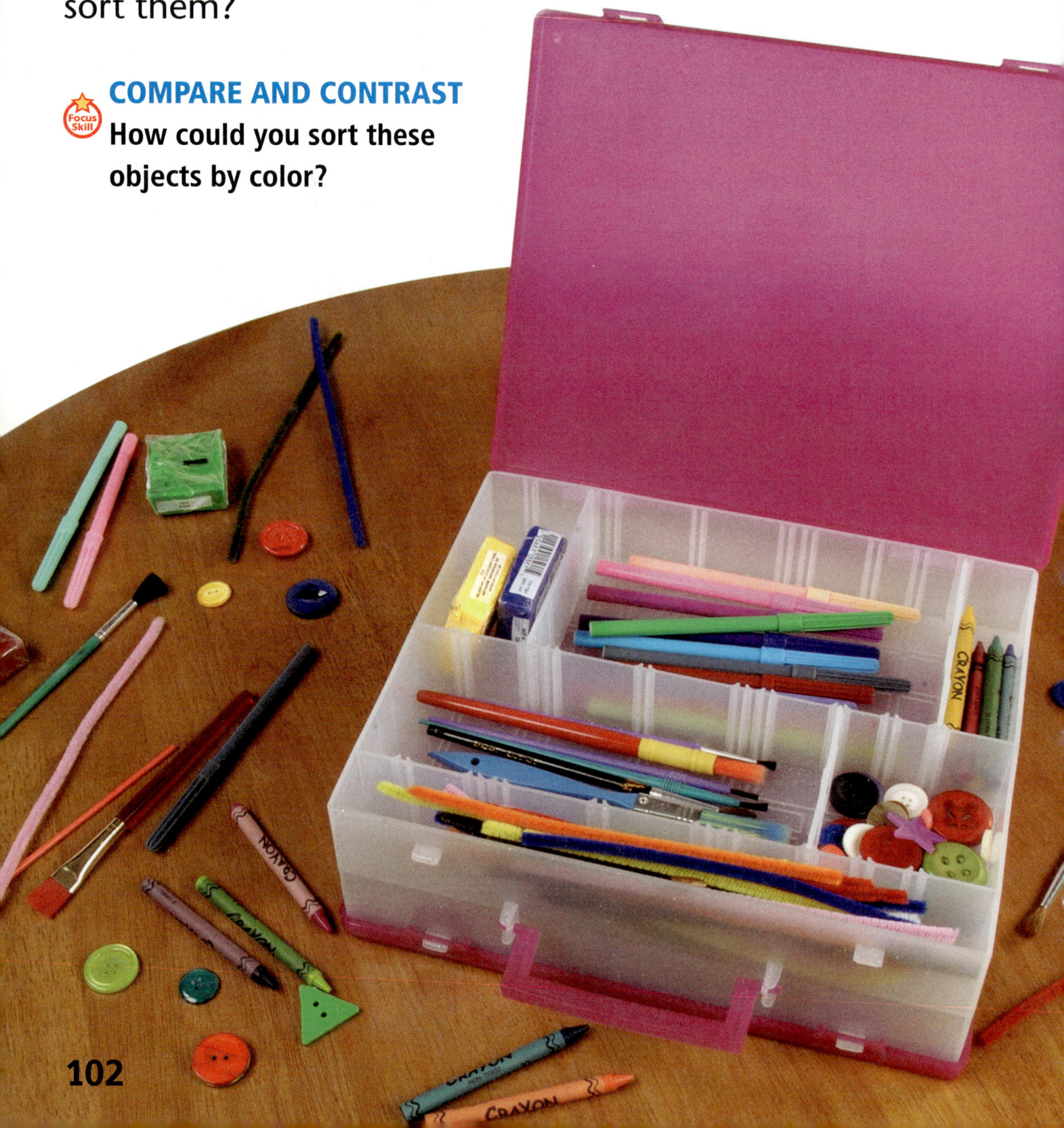

Reading Review

1. **COMPARE AND CONTRAST** Copy and complete this chart.

Matter

alike

Ⓐ _____ is matter.

different

Matter can be different **Ⓑ** _____, such as red and yellow.

Matter can be different sizes, such as **Ⓒ** _____ and **Ⓓ** _____.

Matter can be different **Ⓔ** _____, such as circles and squares.

2. **SUMMARIZE** Write two sentences. Tell how matter can be alike and different.

3. **VOCABULARY** Tell about the **matter** in this picture.

Test Prep

4. Which is true about matter?
   A. It is all the same color.
   B. It is all the same size.
   C. It is only soft things.
   D. Everything is matter.

Links

Writing

Labeling Matter

Use self-stick notes to make labels for matter in your classroom. On each label, name the matter. Then write three words that tell about it.

For more links and activities, go to www.hspscience.com

103

Lesson 2

What Can We Observe About Solids?

Fast Fact

These animals are made of millions of toy blocks. You can compare toys in many ways.

Investigate

Measuring Mass

You need

• 2 blocks

• balance

Step 1

Put a block on each side of the balance.

Step 2

Look at the blocks on the balance. **Compare**.

Step 3

Which block has more mass? Which has less mass?

Inquiry Skill

When you **compare** with a balance, you see how much mass things have.

105

Reading in Science

VOCABULARY
solid
mixture
length
mass

 READING FOCUS SKILL

MAIN IDEA AND DETAILS Look for the main ideas about solids.

Observing Solids

How are paper, scissors, and a globe the same? They are all solids.

106

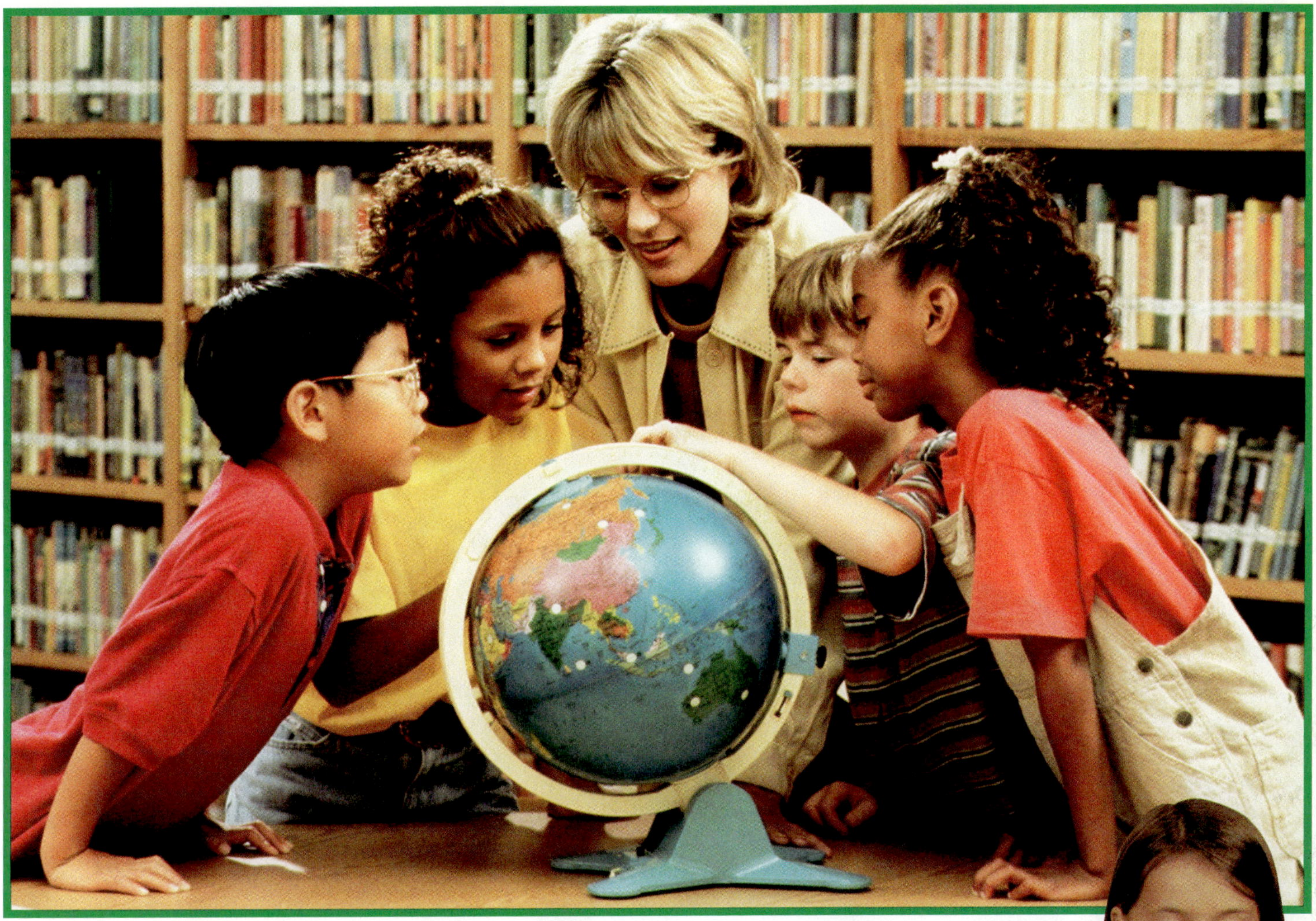

A **solid** is a kind of matter that keeps its shape. It keeps its shape even when you move it.

MAIN IDEA AND DETAILS
Focus Skill
How do you know musical instruments are solids?

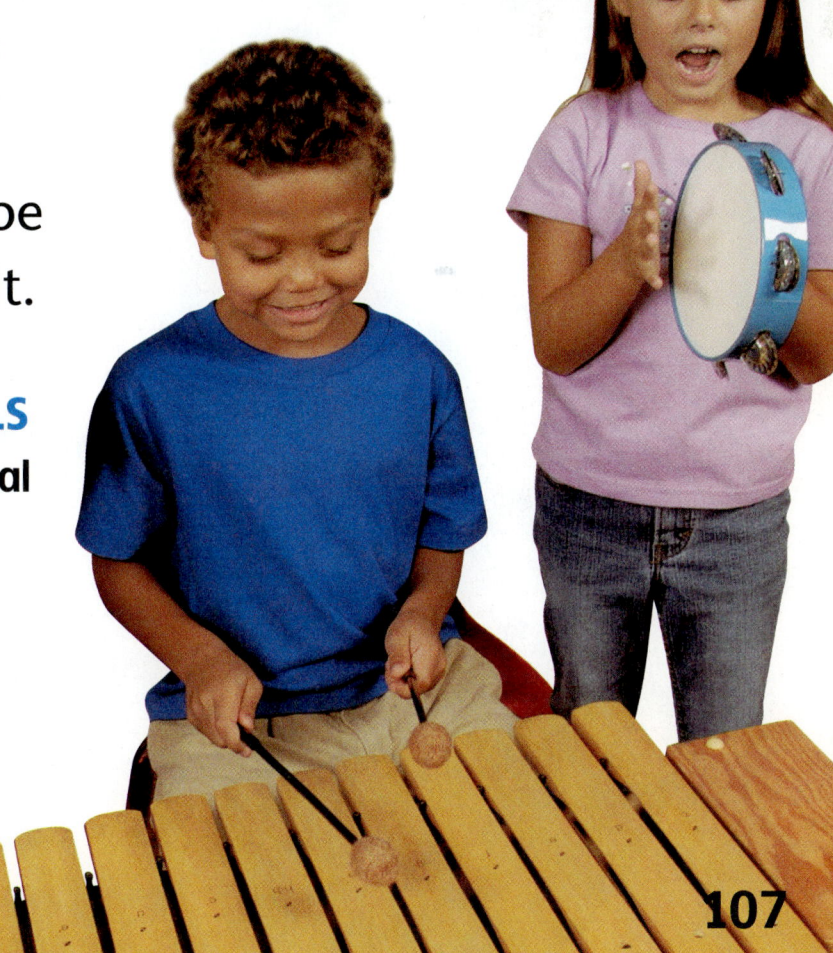

Mixing Solids

When you mix different kinds of matter together, you make a **mixture**. A mixture is made up of two or more things. These drawing tools make a mixture of solids.

The things in a mixture do not change. You can sort them back out of the mixture.

 MAIN IDEA AND DETAILS
What is a mixture made up of?

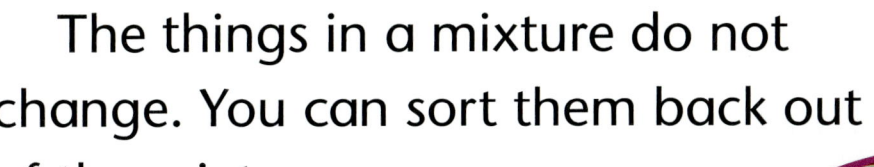

This boy sorts the tools in the mixture.

Make Mixtures

Get small things from the classroom. Mix them together. Then trade mixtures with a partner. Sort the things back out of each other's mixtures.

109

Measuring Solids

You can measure solids. You can measure how long a solid is. That is its **length**. You measure length with a ruler.

ruler

You can measure the mass of a solid. **Mass** is the amount of matter a solid has. You measure mass with a balance.

⭐ **MAIN IDEA AND DETAILS** What are two ways you can measure solids?

balance

Reading Review

1. **MAIN IDEA AND DETAILS** Copy and complete this chart.

   Solids

   Main Idea
   A solid is matter that keeps its shape.

   detail
   You can mix solids.

   detail
   You can Ⓐ _____ solids.

2. **DRAW CONCLUSIONS** How do you know a pencil is a solid?

3. **VOCABULARY** Tell about the **mass** of these blocks.

Test Prep

4. Write a sentence about two solids you see. Tell how they are alike.

Links

Math

Measure Length

Find three small objects in your classroom. Use paper clips to measure their lengths. Record the lengths in a bar graph. Which object is the longest?

 For more links and activities, go to www.hspscience.com

111

Lesson 3

What Can We Observe About Liquids?

Fast Fact

Water is all around you. More than half of your body is water! You can measure water with tools.

Investigate

The Shape of Liquids

You need

- 3 containers of water
- measuring cup

Step 1

Look at the containers. Draw their shapes.

Step 2

Predict which container will have the most water.

Step 3

Measure the water in each container. Was your prediction right?

Inquiry Skill

When you **measure** something, you use tools to learn about it.

113

Reading in Science

VOCABULARY
liquid
dissolve
float
sink

 READING FOCUS SKILL

MAIN IDEA AND DETAILS Look for main ideas about liquids.

Observing Liquids

How are the soap and water alike? Both are liquids.

A **liquid** is matter that flows. It does not have its own shape. It takes the shape of its container.

MAIN IDEA AND DETAILS
What is a liquid?

liquid soap

water

114

Liquid Mixtures

You can make mixtures with liquids. You can mix drink powder or salt with water. They **dissolve**, or mix completely with the liquid.

If you mix soil or oil with water, they do not dissolve.

MAIN IDEA AND DETAILS How can you tell if something dissolves?

Float and Sink

Does matter float or sink? You can test it.

Some objects **float**, or stay on top of a liquid.

Which objects sink?

Some objects **sink**, or fall to the bottom of a liquid.

MAIN IDEA AND DETAILS How can you find out if matter floats or sinks?

Insta-Lab

What Floats?
Get a coin, a pencil, and other classroom objects. Predict which ones will float. Then fill a large bowl with water. Put each object in the water. Were your predictions right?

Measuring Liquids

You can measure liquids. You can use a measuring cup to find out how much space a liquid takes up. You can use a balance to measure its mass.

MAIN IDEA AND DETAILS How can you measure liquids?

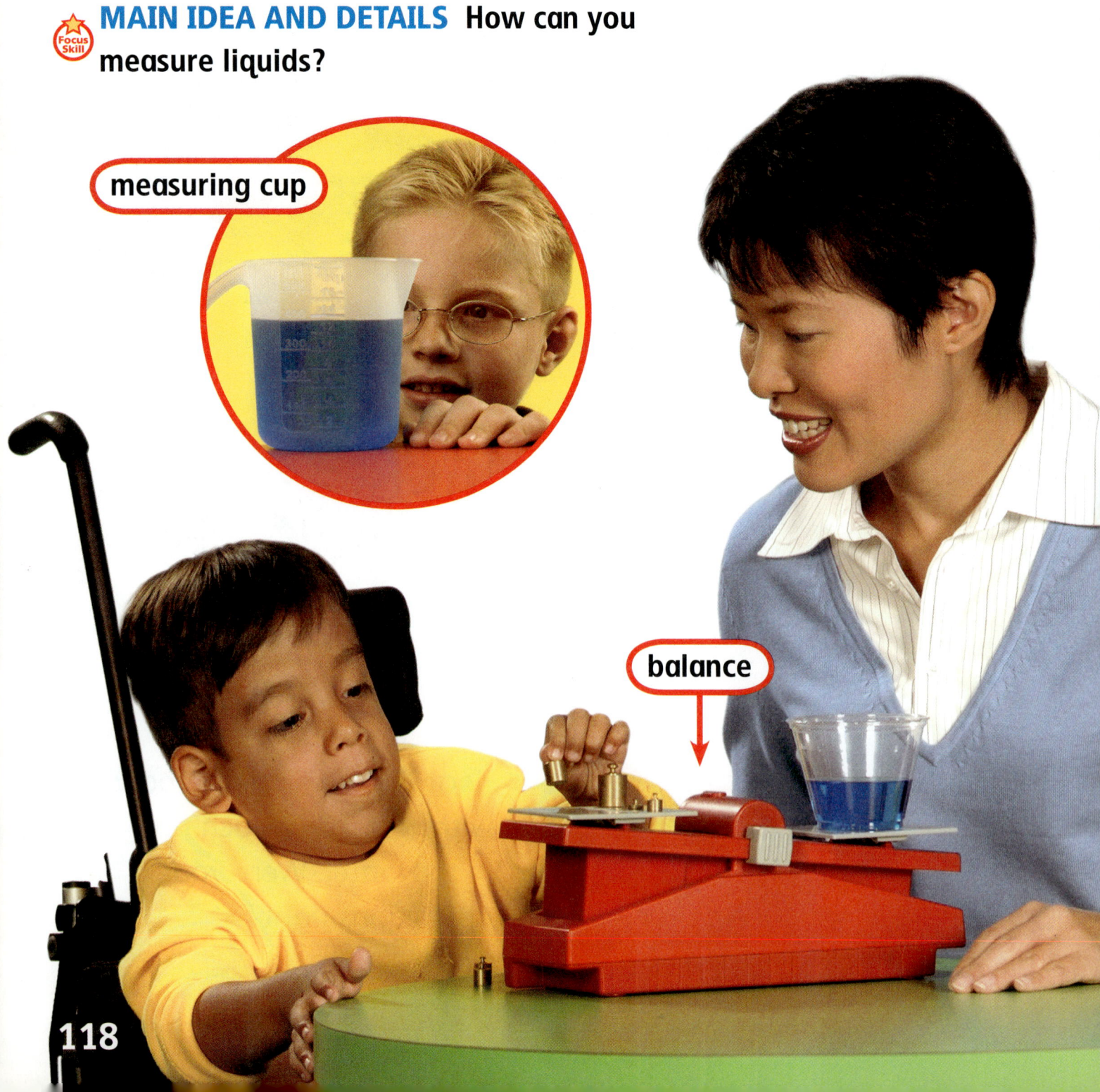

measuring cup

balance

Reading Review

 1. **MAIN IDEA AND DETAILS** Copy and complete this chart.

```
        Liquids

       Main Idea
A liquid is matter that Ⓐ _____.
It Ⓑ _____ its own shape.

    detail                    detail
Some matter dissolves     Some matter Ⓒ _____, and
in liquids.               some floats.
```

2. **SUMMARIZE** Use the chart to write a lesson summary.

3. **VOCABULARY** Use **sink** and **float** to talk about this picture.

Test Prep

4. Which tool would you use to measure the mass of a liquid?
   A. a balance
   B. a hand lens
   C. a pen
   D. a ruler

Links

Health

Healthful Liquids

Draw pictures of liquids people can drink. Sort them into two groups—good for you and not good for you. Talk about why you sorted them as you did.

 **For more links and activities**, go to www.hspscience.com

119

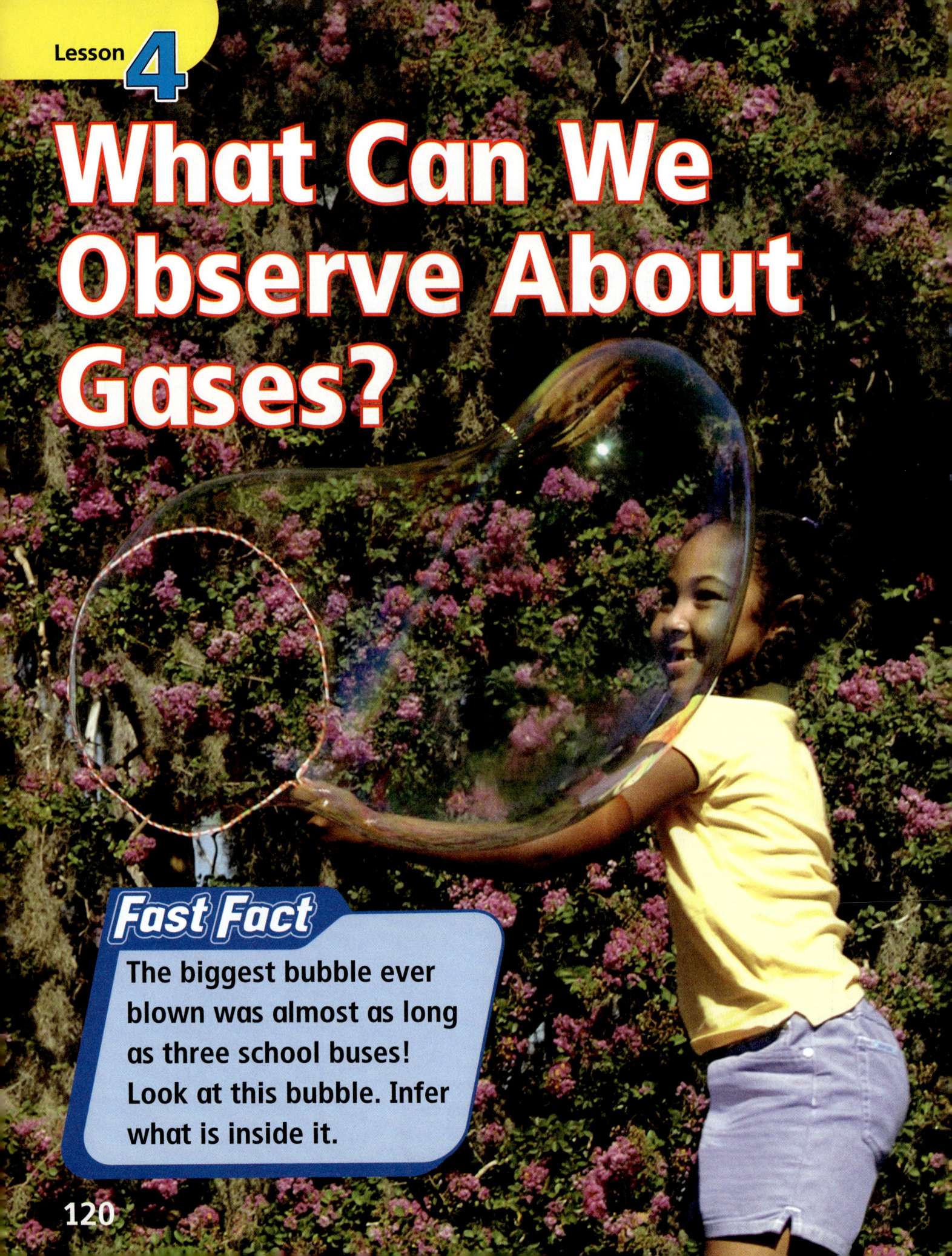

Lesson 4

What Can We Observe About Gases?

Fast Fact

The biggest bubble ever blown was almost as long as three school buses! Look at this bubble. Infer what is inside it.

Investigate

Matter in a Bottle

You need

- clean plastic bottle
- balloon

Step 1

Squeeze the bottle. Blow up the balloon. Observe the air coming out of each.

Step 2

Put the balloon in the bottle. Pull the end around the top. Try to blow up the balloon.

Step 3

What happened? **Infer** what else is in the bottle.

Inquiry Skill

When you **infer**, you use what you observed to tell why something happened.

Reading in Science

VOCABULARY
gas
steam

 **READING FOCUS SKILL**
CAUSE AND EFFECT Think about how and why matter may change.

Observing Gases

Air is made of gases. A gas is a kind of matter. You can not see most gases.

Where is the air in each picture?

122

A **gas** is matter that does not have its own shape. It spreads out to fill its container. It takes the shape of the container.

CAUSE AND EFFECT What would happen if you blew air into a bag? Why?

 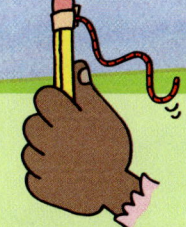

A Wind Hunt

Did you know that wind is moving air? Go on an air hunt. Tape yarn to the end of a pencil. Hold it near heaters, windows, and doors. Observe the yarn. What makes it move?

Heating and Cooling Matter

Heating and cooling can change matter. You can see how matter changes by observing water.

In summer the water in this stream is warm. This keeps the water liquid.

water

In winter the water in the stream gets cold. When the water gets cold enough, it changes into ice. Ice is solid water.

In spring the water will get warm again. It will change back into a liquid.

CAUSE AND EFFECT What changes water from a liquid to a solid?

ice

Science Up Close

What Is Steam?

When water boils, it becomes a gas. This gas is called **steam**.

1 When the water gets hot enough, it becomes steam. The steam goes into the air.

2 As steam cools, it forms tiny drops of water that make a little cloud.

For more links and activities, go to www.hspscience.com

Reading Review

1. **CAUSE AND EFFECT** Copy and complete this chart.

Changes in Matter

cause → effect

- Water is **A** _____. → Water is a liquid.
- Water is very cold. → Water changes into a **B** _____.
- Water is very **C** _____. → Water changes into a gas.

2. **DRAW CONCLUSIONS** Is ice a gas? How do you know?

3. **VOCABULARY** Use the word **steam** to tell about the picture.

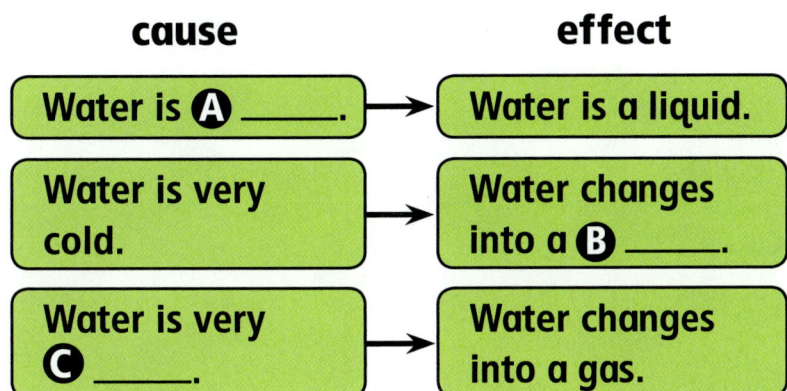

Test Prep

4. Write sentences to tell how matter can change.

Links

Art

Make a Mobile

Make a mobile with art supplies, string, and a plastic hanger. Hang it near a window or door. Watch how air moves the objects on the mobile.

 For more links and activities, go to www.hspscience.com

127

Cleaning Up Oil

Oil spills can happen when a boat carrying oil hits something. Oil is liquid that does not mix with water. It floats on water.

Oil pollutes water in oceans, lakes, or rivers. It also hurts animals. Scientists worked to find ways to clean up oil spills.

When oil spills into the ocean, it is very hard to clean up. Workers must use special soap and sponges to clean up the oil.

THINK ABOUT IT

How can oil spills harm the environment?

Well Oiled

Oil is a heavy, sticky liquid. Some of it is even used to heat houses.

Find out more! Log on to www.hspscience.com

129

Making Protective Packages

Have you ever opened a milk carton and a bad smell came out? That is because the milk turned sour. Milk turns sour after about 14 days.

A scientist named Manuel Marquez Sanchez has made a new kind of milk carton. This new carton changes color. It changes color when the milk inside it is turning sour. Sanchez is also trying to make other food packages better.

SCIENCE Projects for Home or School
You Can Do It!

Materials
- water
- 2 ice cube trays
- freezer

Explore Cooling
What to Do
1. Fill both trays with water.
2. Put one tray in a freezer. Put the other on a table.
3. Wait a few hours. Then look at each tray. What happened?

Draw Conclusions
How did the liquid water change in the freezer? Why?

Mixtures All Around
Many things are mixtures. Choose a mixture in your classroom. Draw it. Then look for the different kinds of matter that are in it. Label each kind. Compare your drawing with a classmate's.

Chapter 3 Review and Test Preparation

Vocabulary Review

Tell which picture goes best with each word.

1. **solid** p. 107
2. **mass** p. 110
3. **liquid** p. 114
4. **float** p. 116

A.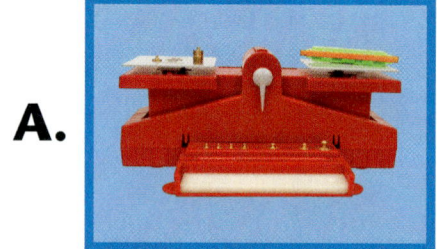

B.

C.

D.

Check Understanding

5. Tell why this is a mixture.

6. Which is a liquid?
   A. air
   B. clay
   C. milk
   D. paper

Critical Thinking

7. What **causes** the stream to change from a solid to a liquid?

8. Think of a solid object. How could you measure it? Write a plan.

133

Enrichment Chapter

4 Heat, Light, and Sound

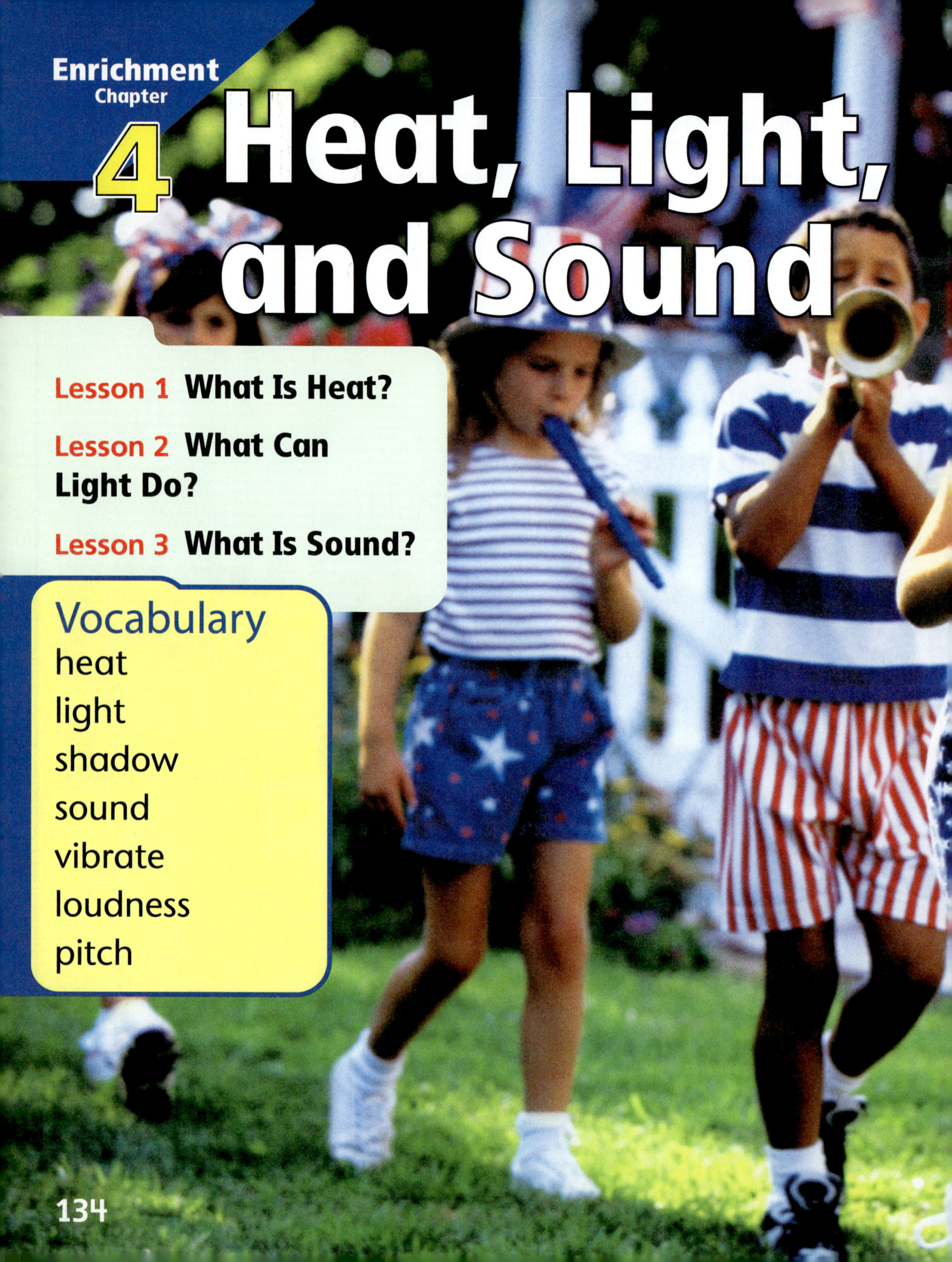

Lesson 1 **What Is Heat?**

Lesson 2 **What Can Light Do?**

Lesson 3 **What Is Sound?**

Vocabulary
heat
light
shadow
sound
vibrate
loudness
pitch

I wonder...

Why do musical instruments make different sounds?

What do you wonder?

Lesson 1

What Is Heat?

Fast Fact

The sun is made of very, very hot gases. Its heat warms Earth. You can plan an investigation to find out how the sun warms Earth.

Investigate

Heat from the Sun

You need

- cup of soil

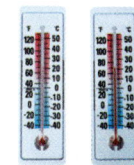
- 2 thermometers

Step 1

Does the sun warm soil faster than it warms air? **Plan an investigation** to find out. Write your **plan**.

Step 2

Follow your **plan** to **investigate** your ideas.

Step 3

Share with the class what you learned.

Inquiry Skill

You **plan an investigation** by thinking of ideas and trying them out.

137

Reading in Science

VOCABULARY
heat

 READING FOCUS SKILL

CAUSE AND EFFECT Look for all the effects heat has on things.

Heat

Heat is energy that makes things hot. Heat from the sun warms the land, air, and water all around you.

The sun warms land, air, and water.

Some things warm up faster than others. Dark-colored things warm up quickly in the sun. Light-colored things take longer to warm up.

CAUSE AND EFFECT

Focus Skill

What can cause something to warm up quickly?

Insta-Lab

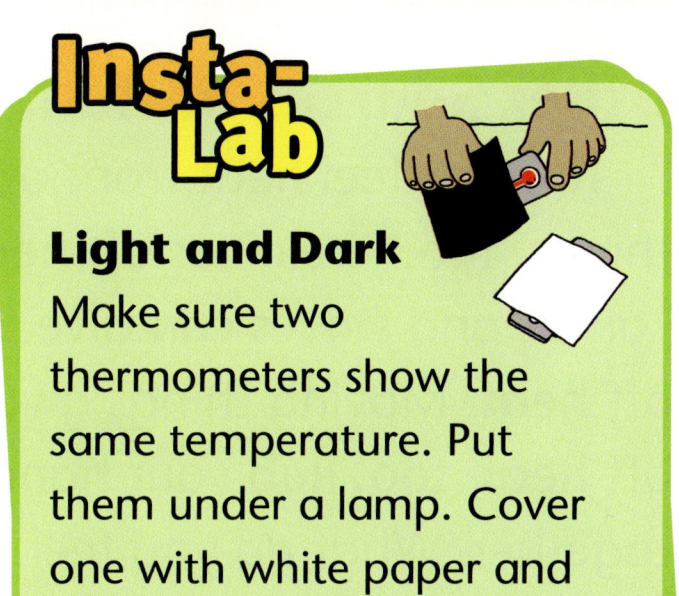

Light and Dark

Make sure two thermometers show the same temperature. Put them under a lamp. Cover one with white paper and one with black paper. Wait 10 minutes. Read the thermometers again. What happened?

Which part of the street gets hot faster?

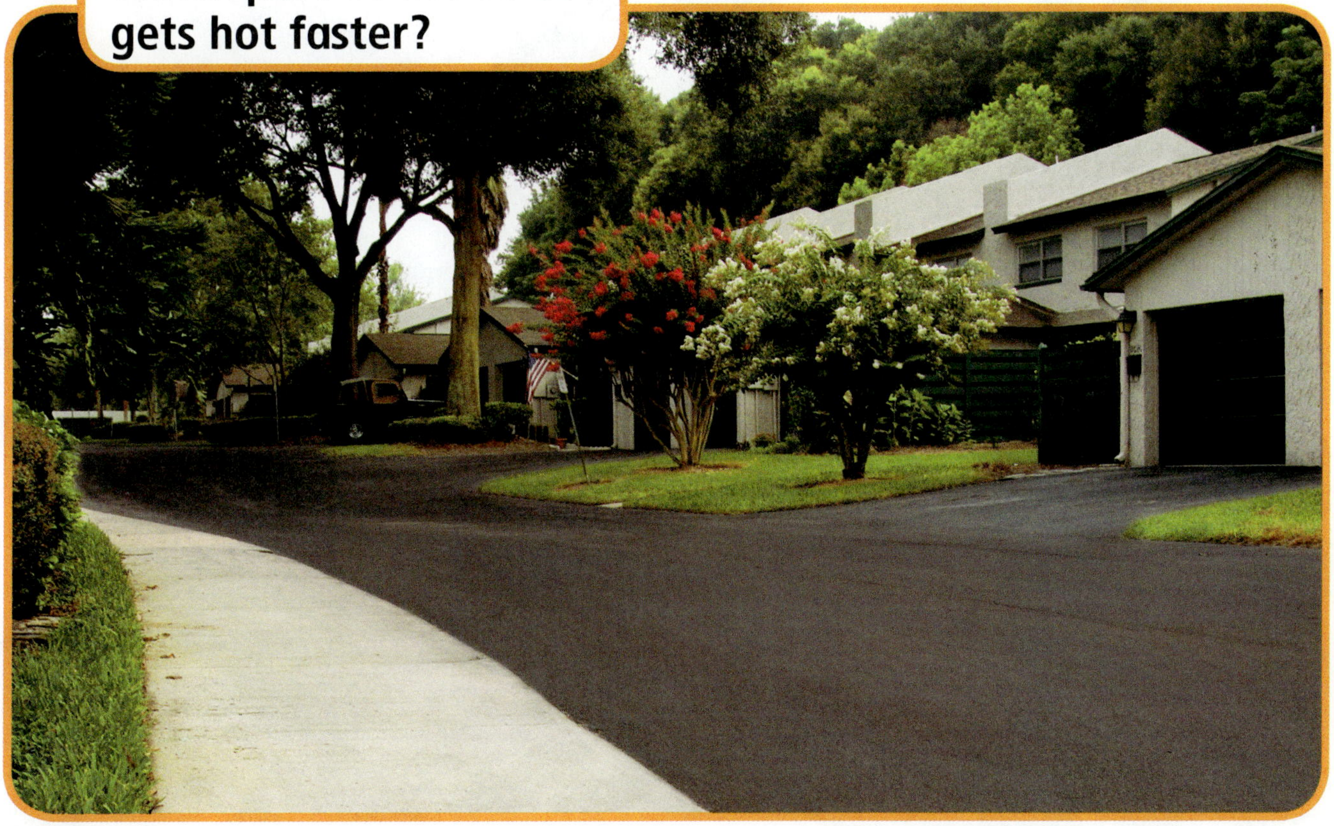

Other Sources of Heat

You can feel heat from other things, too. Fire gives off heat. Lamps and stoves can give off heat. Moving things give off heat, too. Rub your hands together. What do you feel?

CAUSE AND EFFECT What happens when you rub your hands together?

lamp

fire

stove

friction from rubbing hands

Reading Review

1. **CAUSE AND EFFECT** Copy and complete this chart.

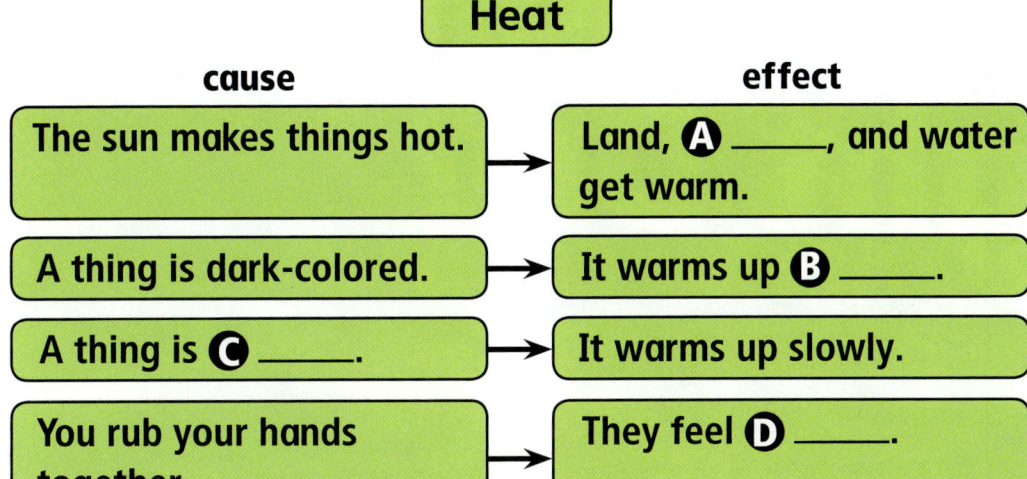

2. **SUMMARIZE** Use the chart to summarize this lesson.

3. **VOCABULARY** Tell about the **heat** in this picture.

Test Prep

4. Which things warm up fastest?
   - A. big things
   - B. cold things
   - C. dark-colored things
   - D. light-colored things

Links

Writing

Report

Read about the sun. Then write a short report about it. Tell what it is and where it is. Tell what the sun is made of and what it does. Draw pictures to go with your report.

 For more links and activities, go to www.hspscience.com

141

Lesson 2

What Can Light Do?

Fast Fact

A shadow has a shape like the object that made it. Draw a conclusion about how shadows are made.

Investigate

Look at Shadows

You need
- pencil
- clay
- paper
- crayon

Step 1

Put a pencil in clay.
Put it on the paper.
Put it in a sunny place.

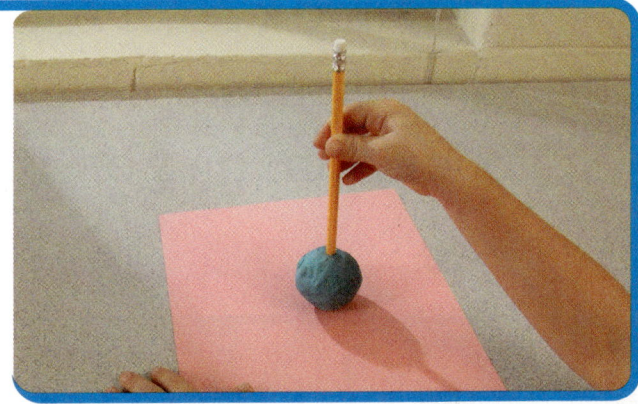

Step 2

Trace the shadow you see on the paper. Then trace it at two other times of the day.

Step 3

Draw a conclusion about why the shadow changed.

Inquiry Skill

To **draw a conclusion**, use what you observed and what you already know.

143

Reading in Science

VOCABULARY
light
shadow

 READING FOCUS SKILL

MAIN IDEA AND DETAILS Look for the main ideas about light and what it does.

Light

Light is a kind of energy. Light from the sun lights up the world around us. Fire and lamps give off light, too. Light lets us see.

sunlight

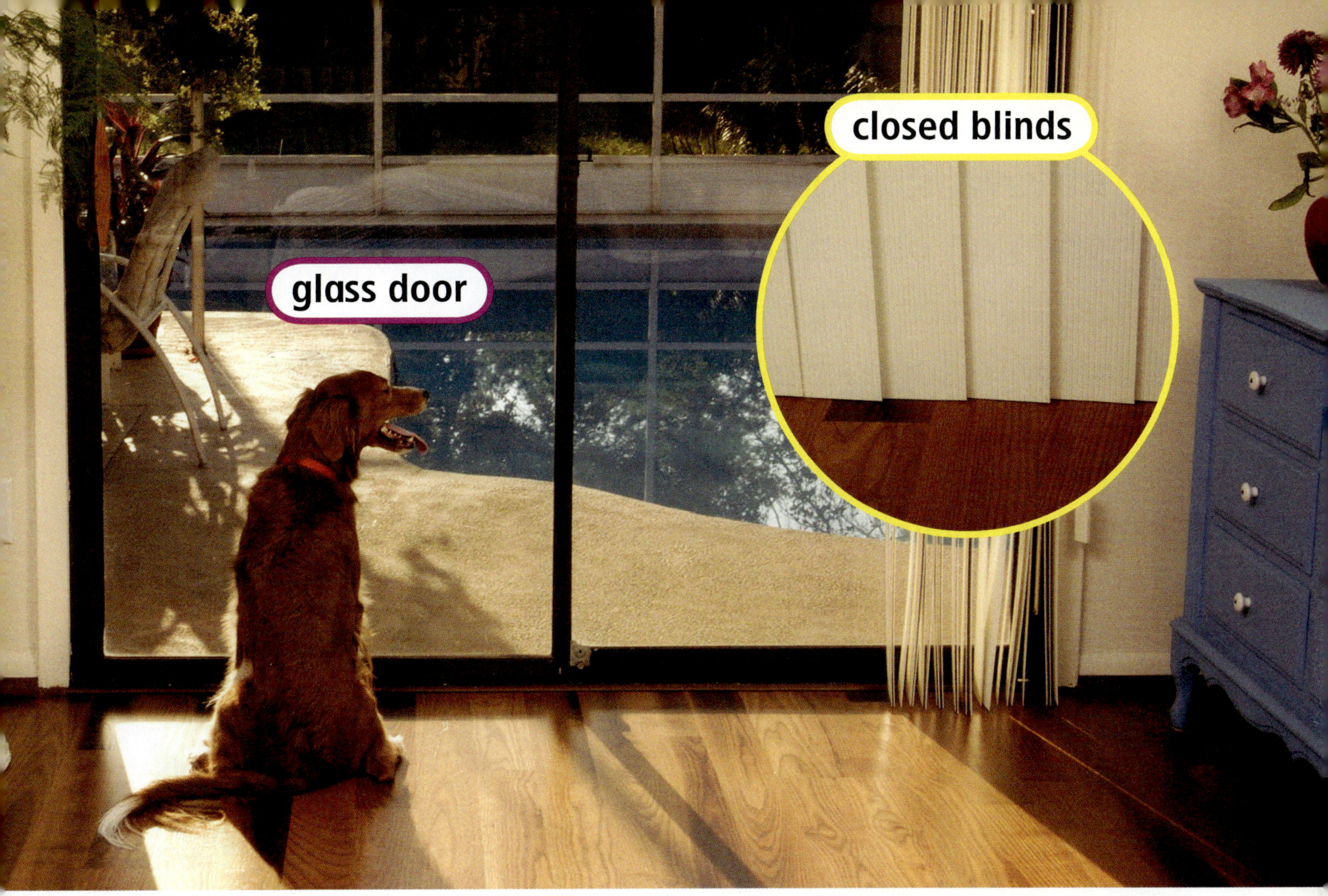
closed blinds
glass door

Light can move. It can pass through clear objects. It passes through glass. Light can not pass through all objects. Objects that are not clear block light.

MAIN IDEA AND DETAILS
Focus Skill
What is the main thing light does for us?

Insta-Lab

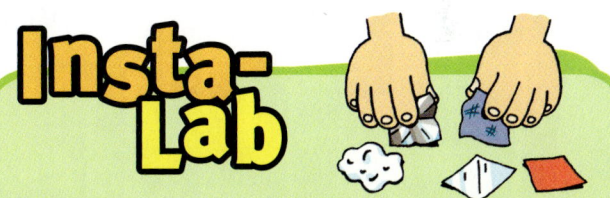

What Can Light Pass Through?

Get some art materials. Predict which ones light will pass through. Which ones will block light? Test your ideas in a sunny place or next to a lamp. **CAUTION:** A lamp may get hot.

Shadows

A **shadow** is a dark place made when an object blocks light. You can see many shadows on a sunny day.

MAIN IDEA AND DETAILS
What makes shadows?

shadow

shadow

Reading Review

 1. **MAIN IDEA AND DETAILS** Copy and complete this chart.

```
                    Light
                      |
                  Main Idea
             Light is a kind of energy.
```

detail	detail	detail	detail
Light lets us **A** _____.	Light can pass through **B** _____ things.	Light is **C** _____ by things that are not clear.	When something blocks light, you see a dark **D** _____.

2. **DRAW CONCLUSIONS**
   Do you think all things can make shadows? Explain your answer.

3. **VOCABULARY** Use the words **light** and **shadow** to tell about this picture.

Test Prep

4. Name something that light could pass through. Tell why you think it could.

Links

Math

Measure a Shadow

Measure how tall you are. Record the number. Then go outside. Have a partner measure the shadow of you that the sun makes. Record the number. Compare the numbers. Are they the same?

 For more links and activities, go to www.hspscience.com

Lesson 3

What Is Sound?

Fast Fact

Sound can travel across spaces. You can hypothesize about what helps sound travel.

Investigate

Watching Sound

You need

- rice
- bowl with foil
- pan
- spoon

Step 1

Put a little rice on the foil. **Hypothesize**. Tell what you think will happen to the rice if you make a loud sound.

Step 2

Hold the pan next to the bowl. Tap it once with the spoon. Observe the rice.

Step 3

Was your **hypothesis** right? Talk about it.

Inquiry Skill

To **hypothesize**, tell what you think will happen. Then test your idea.

Reading in Science

VOCABULARY
sound
vibrate
loudness
pitch

 READING FOCUS SKILL

COMPARE AND CONTRAST Look for ways sounds can be alike and different.

How Sounds Are Made

Sound is a kind of energy that you hear. It is made when something vibrates. To **vibrate** is to move quickly back and forth.

What sounds do you think you could hear on this street?

When you strum guitar strings, each string vibrates. It makes a sound that you can hear.

COMPARE AND CONTRAST
How are all sounds alike?

homemade guitar

vibrating strings

guitar

Sounds Are Different

Some sounds are soft, and some are loud. A sound's **loudness** is how loud or soft it is. The jet makes a loud sound. What else makes a loud sound?

Whispers are soft sounds.

Jets make loud sounds.

Some sounds are high. Others are low. A sound's **pitch** is how high or low it is. The big bell has a low pitch. What else has a low pitch?

COMPARE AND CONTRAST
Focus Skill
What is one way sounds may be different?

Insta-Lab

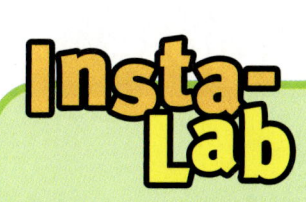

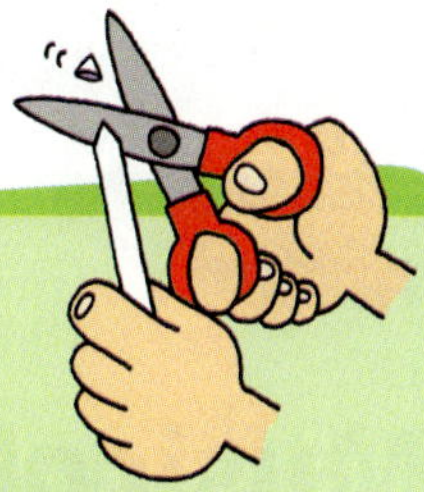

Straw Instrument

Cut a straw so that the top forms a V. Pinch the top with your lips. Blow very hard. Listen. Then cut some of the bottom off the straw. Blow again. How does the sound change?

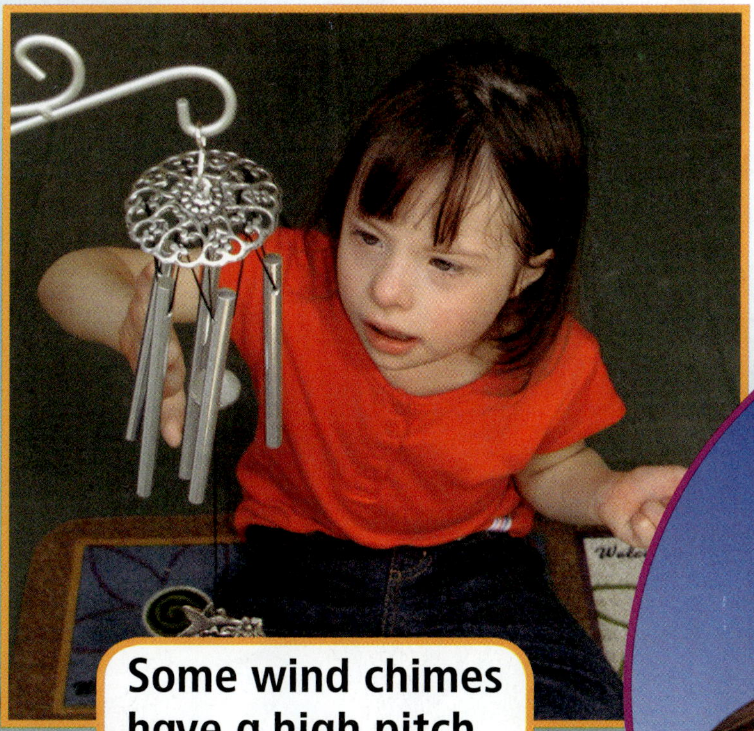

Some wind chimes have a high pitch.

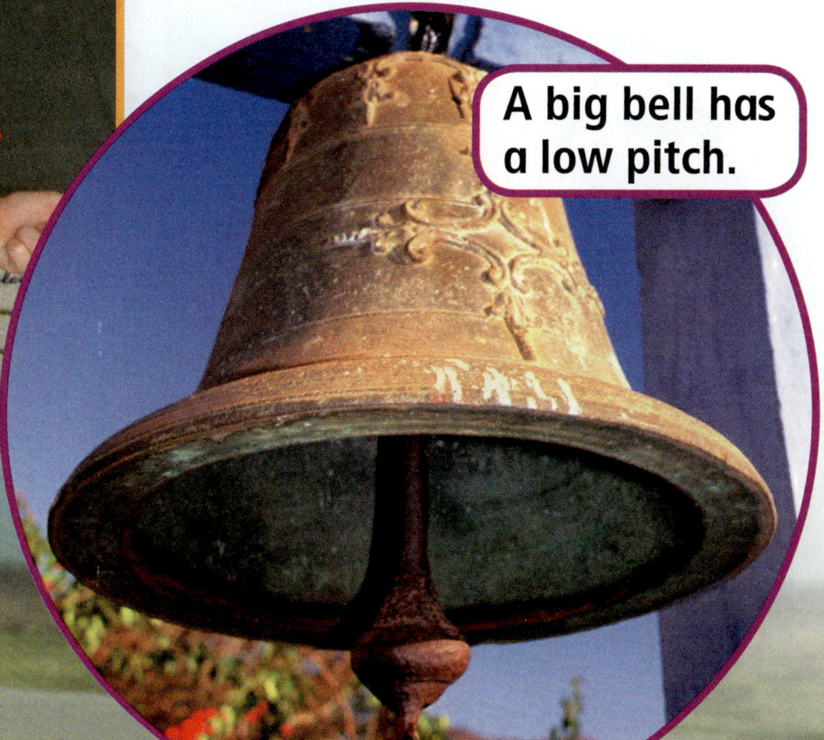

A big bell has a low pitch.

Science Up Close

Musical Instruments

Musical instruments are objects people use to make music. Each kind of instrument causes air to vibrate to make sounds.

When you blow into a trumpet, air vibrates in its metal tubes.

A saxophone has a wooden part called a reed. The reed vibrates, as does the air inside the instrument.

A violin has strings that vibrate.

A drum has a tough cover that vibrates.

For more links and activities, go to www.hspscience.com

Reading Review

 1. COMPARE AND CONTRAST Copy and complete this chart.

Sound

alike

All sounds are made when something **A** _____.

different

A sound's loudness can be loud or **B** _____.

A sound's pitch can be high or **C** _____.

2. SUMMARIZE Use the chart to write a summary of the lesson.

3. VOCABULARY Use the word **vibrate** to tell about the picture.

Test Prep

4. Which is the word for how high or low a sound is?
   A. instrument
   B. loudness
   C. pitch
   D. vibrate

Links

Music

Voice Vibrations

Your throat has parts that help you talk and sing. Sing high. Sing low. Sing loudly. Sing softly. As you sing, feel your throat. Put your other hand near your lips. Write about what you observe.

 For more links and activities, go to www.hspscience.com

155

Technology

How Cell Phones Work

Have you seen kids with cell phones? A cell phone is really a radio. It turns the sound of your voice into another kind of energy. This energy then travels through the air until it reaches a tower.

Dialing Out

The tower picks up the energy. Then the tower sends it out to the number you dialed.

The other person's phone turns the energy back into sound. Did you ever think you would be talking through the air?

THINK ABOUT IT

What does a cell phone do to your voice when you talk into it?

Find out more! Log on to www.hspscience.com

Lighting the World

Thomas Alva Edison was a scientist. He was also an inventor. As a boy he did not hear well. He spent a lot of time reading. Edison loved to read the many science books his mother gave him.

Edison made a special light bulb. The bulb had a special thread inside of it. It could stay lit longer than other light bulbs. Soon his light bulb glowed in many places. Thomas Edison had changed our world.

SCIENCE Projects for Home or School
You Can Do It!

Investigate Pitch
What to Do

1. Blow across the open top of a bottle. Listen. Predict how the sound will change if you put water in the bottle.
2. Put a different amount in each bottle. Blow across the four bottles.
3. Which have a high pitch? Which have a low pitch? Arrange the bottles from highest to lowest pitch.

Materials
- four bottles
- water

Draw Conclusions

What vibrates in an empty bottle to make sound? What effect does adding water have on the sound?

Sun Catcher

Cut out shapes from art materials. Glue them to a sheet of clear colored material. Then hang the sheet in a sunny window. Watch your sun catcher.

Chapter 4

Review and Test Preparation

Vocabulary Review

Match each word to its picture.

1. **heat** p. 138   A.

2. **light** p. 144   B.

3. **shadow** p. 146   C.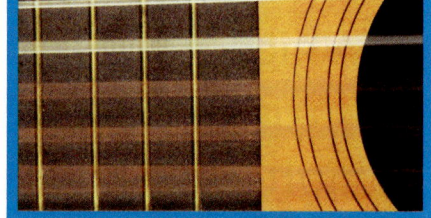

4. **vibrate** p. 150   D.

Check Understanding

5. What **causes** some things to warm up faster than others?

6. Which clothes are good to wear on a hot day? Tell why.

7. Which kind of pitch does a whistle have?

   A. high
   B. loud
   C. low
   D. soft

Critical Thinking

8. Look at this musical instrument. What parts vibrate to make sounds? How do you know?

UNIT 3
Weather and Seasons

EARTH SCIENCE

Chapter 5	Measuring Weather
Chapter 6	Seasons
Chapter 7	Objects in the Sky

Spring Maple-Sugaring Festival

TO: colton@hspscience.com
FROM: emily@hspscience.com
RE: Massachusetts

Dear Colton,
I got to see how maple syrup is made. In the spring, sap is collected from the trees and is boiled. It tastes good on pancakes!
Emily

162

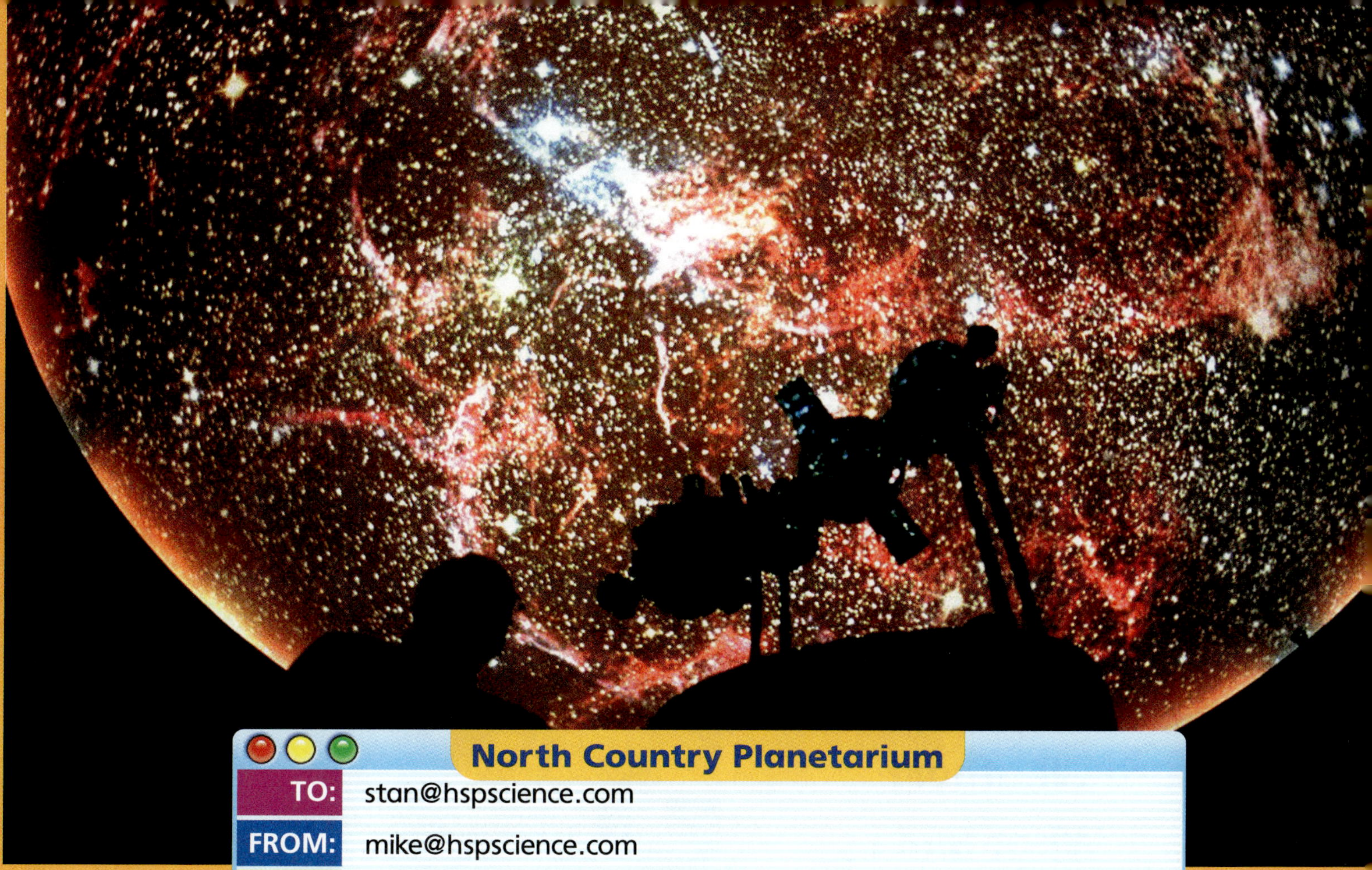

North Country Planetarium

TO: stan@hspscience.com

FROM: mike@hspscience.com

RE: Plattsburgh State University

Dear Stan,

I saw the moon and the stars. I was not outside. I was inside a planetarium. Do you like to look for objects in the sky?

Your friend,

Mike

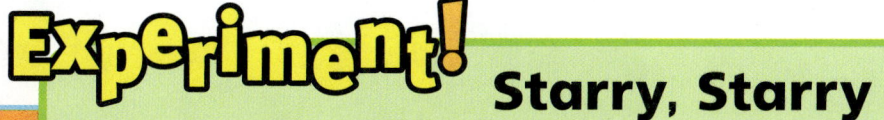

Experiment! Starry, Starry Night

As you do this unit, you will find out about objects in the sky. Plan and do a test. Find out how the nighttime sky is different from the daytime sky.

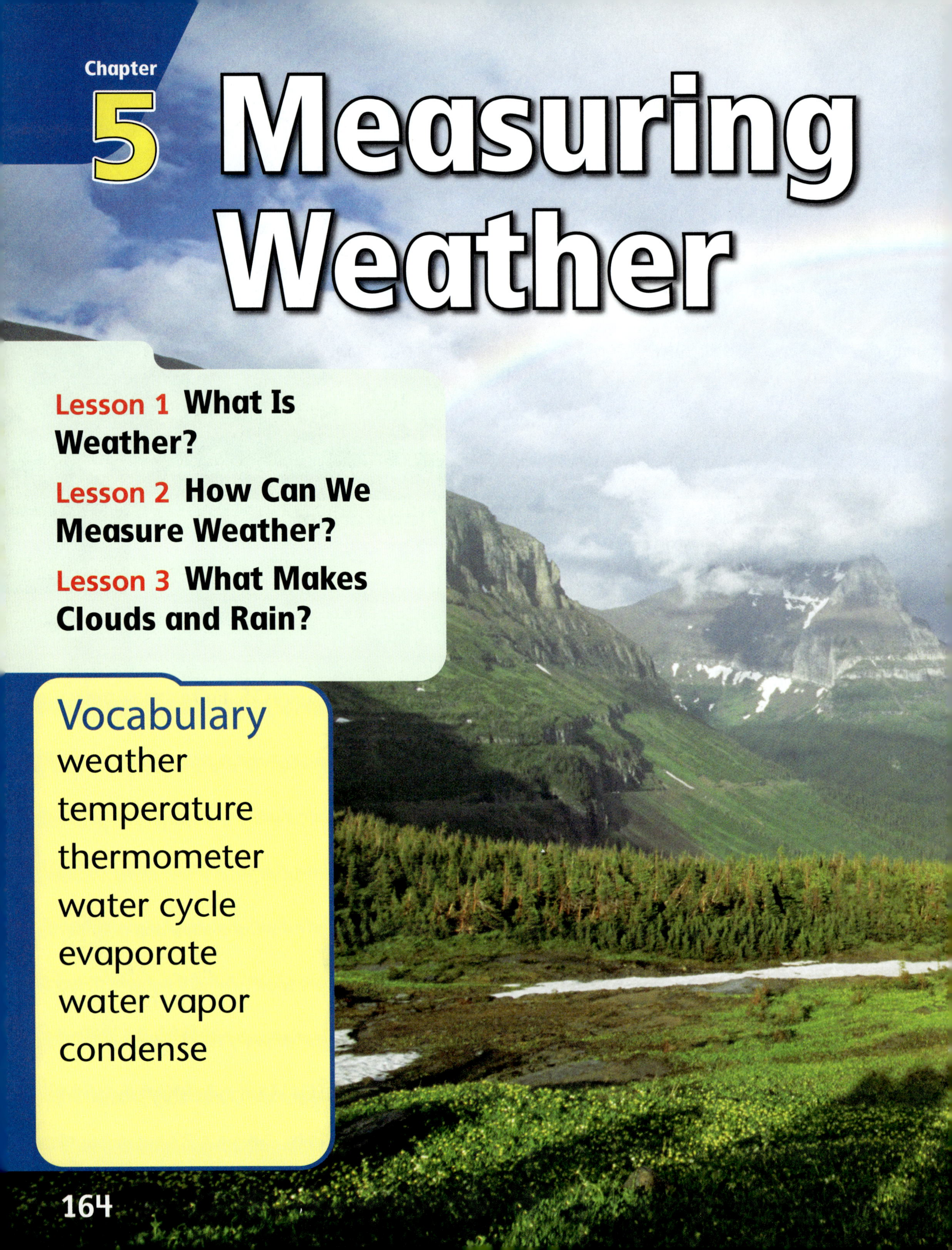

Chapter 5 Measuring Weather

Lesson 1 What Is Weather?

Lesson 2 How Can We Measure Weather?

Lesson 3 What Makes Clouds and Rain?

Vocabulary

weather
temperature
thermometer
water cycle
evaporate
water vapor
condense

I wonder...
What makes a rainbow?
What do you wonder?

Lesson 1

What Is Weather?

Fast Fact

About 25 centimeters (10 inches) of snow equals about 3 centimeters (1 inch) of rain. You can compare snow to other types of weather.

Investigate

Daily Weather

You need

- paper

- markers

Step 1

Observe the weather each day for two weeks.

Step 2

Make a chart. Record what you see.

Step 3

Compare the weather from day to day. Do you see any patterns? Predict next week's weather.

Inquiry Skill

You can **compare** things by telling how they are alike and how they are different.

Reading in Science

VOCABULARY
weather

 READING FOCUS SKILL
COMPARE AND CONTRAST Look for ways in which weather can be different from day to day.

Weather

Weather is what the air outside is like. You can see and feel the weather. It may be warm or cool. It may be snowy, windy, rainy, cloudy, or sunny.

What weather do you see here?

Weather can change. It may be sunny one day. The next day may be cloudy. It may be cold for many days. Then it may warm up. One day may be windy. Another day may be calm.

COMPARE AND CONTRAST
How can weather be different from day to day?

Insta-Lab

Observing Weather

Look out the window. Observe the sky. Observe what people are wearing. What can you tell about the weather? Repeat each day for a week. Make a chart to show weather data.

Weather and You

You wear heavy clothes in cold weather. You wear light clothes in warm weather. When it rains, you wear clothes that help keep you dry. You may choose activities to go with the weather, too.

COMPARE AND CONTRAST How is clothing for cold weather different from clothing for warm weather?

What activities are these people doing?

Reading Review

1. **COMPARE AND CONTRAST** Copy and complete this chart.

Weather

alike
- All weather is what the **A** _____ outside is like.
- You can see and **C** _____ all weather.

different
- hot, warm, cool, **B** _____
- sunny, **D** _____, rainy, snowy, windy

2. **SUMMARIZE** Write sentences telling the most important parts of this lesson.

3. **VOCABULARY** Write a sentence about **weather**.

Test Prep

4. In which kind of weather do people wear light clothes?
   A. cold
   B. rainy
   C. snowy
   D. warm

Links

Writing

Weather Poem

Think about your favorite kind of weather. Write a poem. Start each line with a letter of a word for that weather. Tell why you like that kind of weather.

 For more links and activities, go to www.hspscience.com

Lesson 2

How Can We Measure Weather?

Fast Fact

This tool shows the direction of the wind. How else do people measure weather?

Investigate

Measure Temperature

You need

- thermometer

- red crayon

Step 1

Draw two thermometers. Label one **inside** and one **outside**.

Step 2

Measure the temperature inside and outside the classroom. Record on the thermometers you drew.

Step 3

How do your **measurements** help you know where it is warmer?

Inquiry Skill

When you **measure** with a thermometer, you find out the temperature.

173

Reading in Science

VOCABULARY
temperature
thermometer

 READING FOCUS SKILL
MAIN IDEA AND DETAILS Look for the main ideas about measuring weather.

Measuring Temperature

One way to measure weather is to find the temperature. **Temperature** is the measure of how hot or cold something is. A **thermometer** is a tool for measuring temperature.

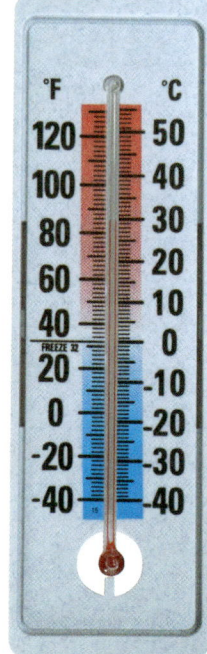

thermometer

 MAIN IDEA AND DETAILS How can you find out how warm the air is outside?

174

Measuring Rain

You can also measure how much rain falls. This tool is a rain gauge. It shows how much rain has fallen.

MAIN IDEA AND DETAILS
How can you measure rain?

rain gauge

Insta-Lab

Where's the Heat?
Find the warmest place in your classroom. Use a thermometer. Measure the temperature in different places. Tell what you find out.

175

Measuring Wind

You can measure wind, too. An anemometer measures the speed of the wind. A weather vane shows the direction of the wind. A windsock also shows the direction of the wind.

MAIN IDEA AND DETAILS
What are two tools that measure the direction of wind?

weather vane

anemometer

windsocks

Reading Review

1. MAIN IDEA AND DETAILS Copy and complete this chart.

Measuring Weather

Main Idea
You can measure weather in many ways.

detail
You can measure **A** _____, which is how hot or cold it is.

detail
You can measure how much **B** _____ has fallen.

detail
You can measure the **C** _____ and **D** _____ of the wind.

2. DRAW CONCLUSIONS
How can measuring weather help people?

3. VOCABULARY
Use the words **temperature** and **thermometer** to tell about the picture.

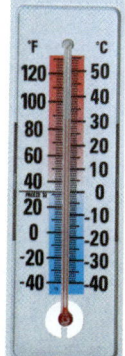

Test Prep

4. What are three ways you can measure weather?

Links

Math

Solve Problems
Juan checked his rain gauge. He saw 5 centimeters of rain on Monday. He saw 3 centimeters more rain on Tuesday. How much rain fell in all?

 For more links and activities, go to www.hspscience.com

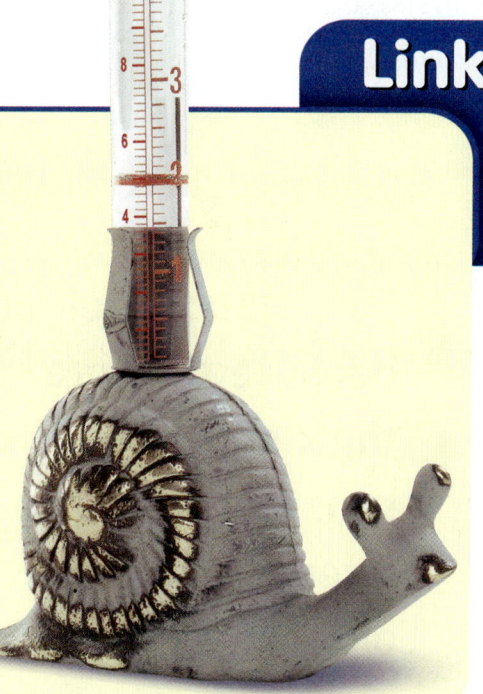

Lesson 3

What Makes Clouds and Rain?

Fast Fact

Rain clouds look dark because they are thick and block the sun. What can you infer about rain and clouds?

Investigate

Make Clouds

You need

 jar with lid    hot water    ice cubes

Step 1

Let your teacher put the hot water in the jar. Wait one minute. Then pour most of it out. **CAUTION:** hot water!

Step 2

Turn the jar lid upside down. Place it on the jar. Observe.

Step 3

Place ice on the lid. Observe. **Infer** how clouds form.

Inquiry Skill

To **infer** what happens, observe carefully. Then draw a conclusion.

179

Reading in Science

VOCABULARY
water cycle
evaporate
water vapor
condense

 READING FOCUS SKILL
CAUSE AND EFFECT Look for what causes clouds and rain to form.

The Water Cycle

Clouds and rain are part of the water cycle. In the **water cycle**, water moves from Earth to the air and back again.

The Water Cycle

1 The sun makes water warm. This causes the water to **evaporate**, or change to water vapor. **Water vapor** is water in the air that you can not see.

2 Water vapor meets cool air. The cool air causes the water vapor to **condense**, or change into tiny water drops. The drops form clouds.

180

3. Water drops come together and get bigger and heavier. Then they fall as rain or snow.

4. Some rain and snow falls into rivers, lakes, and oceans. Some flows there from the land.

5. The cycle continues.

For more links and activities, go to www.hspscience.com

Clouds

Clouds are clues about how the weather may change.

CAUSE AND EFFECT **What kind of clouds bring rain or snow?**

Insta-Lab

Monday
It will be sunny and nice.

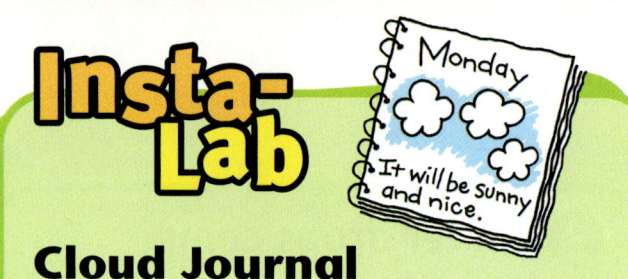

Cloud Journal

Keep a journal of clouds and the weather. Each morning, draw the clouds you see. Predict what the weather will be like. Later, check to see if your predictions were right.

Clouds	Weather
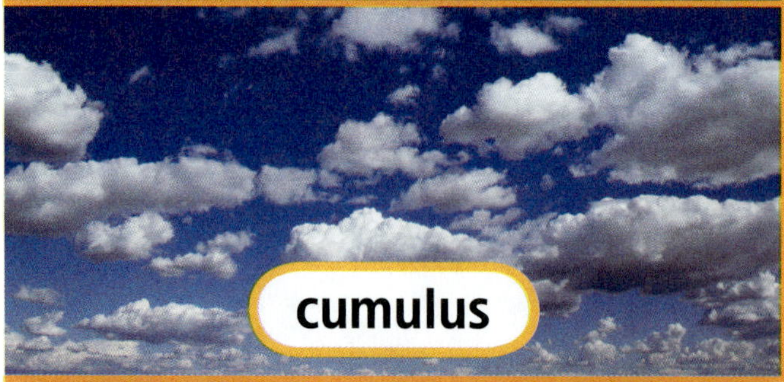 cumulus	Some clouds look like puffy white cotton. They often mean nice weather.
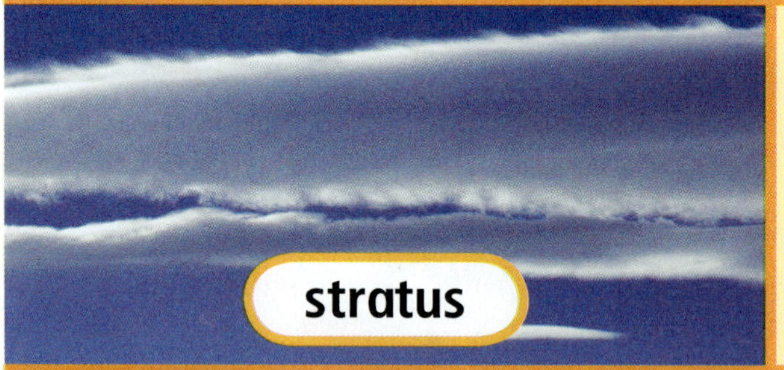 stratus	Other clouds are gray, flat, and low in the sky. They may bring rain or snow.
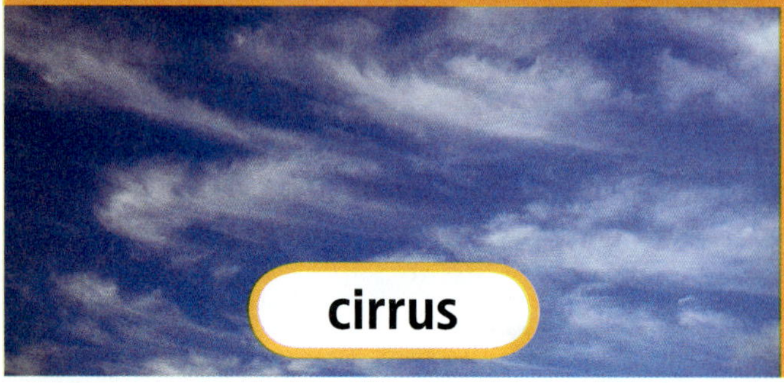 cirrus	These clouds look like thin, white feathers. They often mean sunny weather.

Reading Review

1. **CAUSE AND EFFECT** Copy and complete this chart.

   The Water Cycle

cause	effect
Sun heats water. →	Water **A** _____.
Water vapor meets cool air. →	The cool air makes the water vapor **B** _____.
Water drops get bigger and heavier. →	Then they fall as **C** _____ or **D** _____.

2. **SUMMARIZE** Write a sentence telling the main idea of this lesson.

3. **VOCABULARY** Use the word **condense** to tell about this picture.

Test Prep

4. In what does water move from the land to the air and back again?
   - A. in the water cycle
   - B. in the ocean
   - C. in the clouds
   - D. in the rain

Links

Math

Use Ordinal Numbers

Work with a partner to draw the steps of the water cycle. Write about each step. First, the sun heats the water. Use second, third, and fourth to retell the other steps.

For more links and activities, go to www.hspscience.com

183

Is the Weather Getting Worse?

Earth's weather can get pretty wild. Scientists say that Earth's weather is getting wilder. That's because Earth's temperature is rising.

Using Powerful Tools

Weather experts use satellites to study weather. Satellites with cameras are launched into space. The satellites take pictures showing Earth's weather.

The pictures are sent to weather experts. The experts then use computers. The computers help predict what the weather will be in the future.

Looking Back

Weather experts looked at weather in the past. They compared that weather with today's weather. The experts say the study showed that the world's weather is changing.

Scientists say the change is because Earth's temperature is rising. This change might mean less rain will fall in the future. Or, it may mean that summer weather will last longer.

Warming Warning!

Scientists say that the world's weather will keep getting worse if the warming does not stop.

THINK ABOUT IT

How do satellites help weather experts?

Find out more! Log on to www.hspscience.com

Watching the Weather

Meteorologists are weather scientists. They can tell when the weather will change. They study weather patterns to predict when a thunderstorm might happen. Thunderstorms can bring strong wind and heavy rain. They can harm people and their homes. If people know when bad weather is coming, they can make plans to stay safe. Meteorologists help people do that.

SCIENCE Projects for Home or School
You Can Do It!

Explore Evaporation

Materials
- 2 plastic cups
- water
- tape
- plastic wrap

What to Do
1. Put the same amount of water in each cup. Put a piece of tape on each cup to mark the waterline. Cover one cup tightly with plastic wrap.
2. Put both cups in a warm place.
3. Wait one day. Compare the water in the cups. Talk about what you see.

Draw Conclusions
What happened to the water in each cup? Why do you think that happened?

Weather Safety

Make a poster about weather safety. Show ways you stay safe in different kinds of weather. Tell ways to stay safe in the sun, in snowstorms, and in rainstorms. Share your poster with the class.

Chapter 5

Review and Test Preparation

Vocabulary Review

Use the words below to complete the sentences.

weather p. 168   **evaporate** p. 180
thermometer p. 174   **water vapor** p. 180

1. A tool that measures temperature is a ___.

2. Warmth may cause water to ___.

3. Water in the air is ___.

4. The air outside is ___.

Check Understanding

5. What is the **cause** for each **effect** labeled with an arrow in the water cycle?

6. Which tool would you use to find out how fast the wind is blowing?

A. anemometer

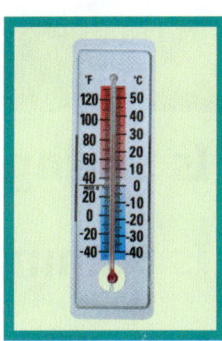

C. thermometer

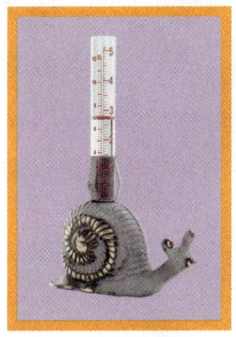

B. rain gauge

D. weather vane

7. What do clouds give clues about?

F. temperature

G. how windy it is

H. how much it will rain

J. what the weather will be

Critical Thinking

8. You are getting dressed for school. How can you make sure you wear the right clothes for the weather?

Chapter 6 Seasons

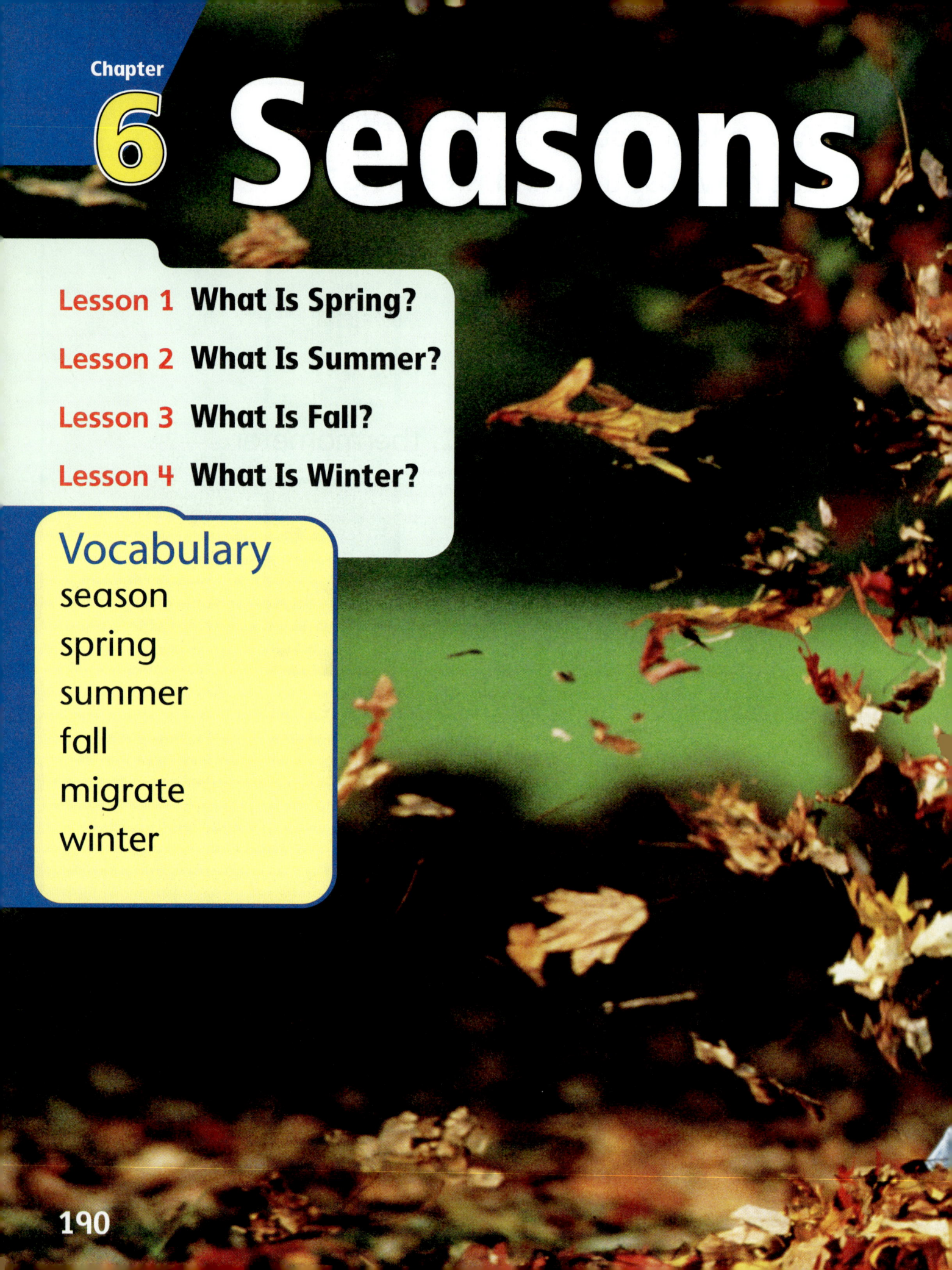

Lesson 1 What Is Spring?

Lesson 2 What Is Summer?

Lesson 3 What Is Fall?

Lesson 4 What Is Winter?

Vocabulary
season
spring
summer
fall
migrate
winter

I wonder...

Why do some leaves change color?

What do you wonder?

Lesson 1

What Is Spring?

Fast Fact

Early spring is the best time to plant a vegetable garden. You can hypothesize about what helps plants grow in spring.

Investigate

Plants and Light

You need

 • young plant    • shoe box with hole    • spray bottle

Step 1

Put the plant in the box. Put the lid on the box.

Step 2

Place the box so that the hole faces a window. **Hypothesize** about what will happen to the plant.

Step 3

Spray the plant with water each day. After one week, what happens? Was your **hypothesis** correct?

Inquiry Skill

When you **hypothesize**, you think of an idea.

193

Reading in Science

VOCABULARY
season
spring

 **READING FOCUS SKILL**
MAIN IDEA AND DETAILS Look for the main ideas about spring.

Seasons

A **season** is a time of year. A year has four seasons. The seasons are spring, summer, fall, and winter. They form a pattern. After every winter comes spring.

Science Up Close

Seasons

Spring starts in the month of March.

194

For more links and activities, go to www.hspscience.com

Spring

Spring is the season after winter. In spring, the weather gets warmer. There may be many rainy days. Spring has more hours of daylight than winter. People may go outside more.

MAIN IDEA AND DETAILS
What is the weather like in spring?

rain

How can you tell it is spring?

Plants in Spring

Many plants begin to grow in spring. They get more warmth, light, and rain in spring than in winter. Plants may grow new leaves and flowers.

MAIN IDEA AND DETAILS
Why do many plants grow well in spring?

Insta-Lab

New Leaves

Take a closer look at new leaves. Use a hand lens to observe a plant stem or a branch. Use a measuring tape too. Observe the size, shape, and color of the new leaves. Talk about how the leaves will change as they grow.

flowers

flowering tree

Animals in Spring

Spring is a good time for many animals to have their young. New plants are food for the young. Some young animals are born. Others hatch from eggs. It is easy for them all to find food.

geese and goslings

MAIN IDEA AND DETAILS
Why is spring a good time for animals to have their young?

ewe and lambs

Reading Review

1. **MAIN IDEA AND DETAILS** Copy and complete this chart.

```
                    Spring

                  Main Idea
          Spring is one of the four seasons.

   detail          detail         detail          detail
The weather     There are      Many plants     Many animals
gets Ⓐ ___      more hours     begin to        have their
in spring.      of Ⓑ ___.      Ⓒ ___.          Ⓓ ___.
```

2. **SUMMARIZE** Use the chart to write a lesson summary.

3. **VOCABULARY** Tell about the **season** in this picture.

Test Prep

4. What helps plants grow in spring?
   A. freezing
   B. seasons
   C. warmth, light, and rain
   D. young animals

Links

Writing

Spring Stories

Write a story about a young animal in spring. Tell about what the animal sees and does. Use what you know about animals in spring to write your story.

 For more links and activities, go to www.hspscience.com

Lesson 2

What Is Summer?

Fast Fact

There are more kinds of shells than you can count. Many people collect shells in summer. You can infer why people do different activities in different seasons.

Investigate

Hot Weather Activities

You need

- seasons picture cards

Step 1

Work with a partner. Talk about what people do in summer.

Step 2

Look at each card. Find clues that tell about the season. **Infer** which pictures show summer.

Step 3

Compare your ideas with other classmates' ideas. How do you know which pictures show summer?

Inquiry Skill

To **infer**, you use what you already know to figure out something.

201

Reading in Science

VOCABULARY
summer

READING FOCUS SKILL
MAIN IDEA AND DETAILS Look for the main ideas about summer.

Summer

Summer is the season after spring. Like spring, it has many hours of daylight. Summer weather can be hot. People wear light clothes. Some places may have thunderstorms.

MAIN IDEA AND DETAILS
What is summer?

hot weather

How can you tell it is summer?

Plants in Summer

Summer weather helps many plants grow. Trees have many green leaves. Some plants grow fruits.

MAIN IDEA AND DETAILS How can plants change in summer?

Insta-Lab

Act Out Summer Activities

Think about things you like to do in summer. Act them out. Ask others to guess what they are. Why is summer a good time to do each thing?

tomato plant

tree with leaves

Animals in Summer

In summer, animals have ways to stay cool. Some cool off in mud or water. Others lose fur so that their coats are lighter.

Young animals can find plants and other food. They grow bigger.

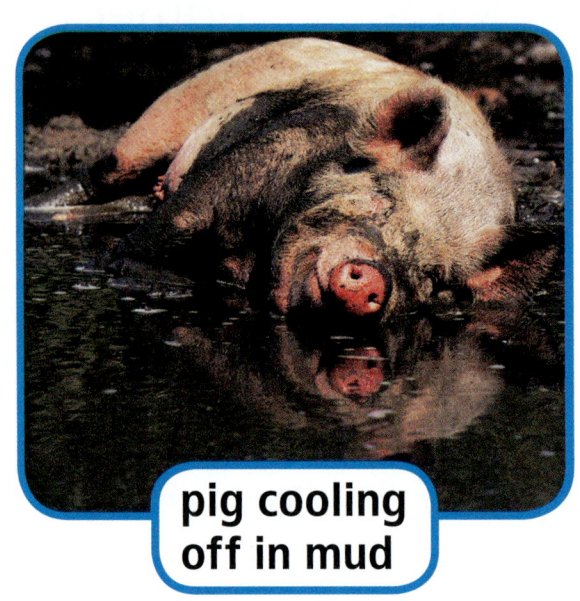

pig cooling off in mud

MAIN IDEA AND DETAILS

Focus Skill

What is one way animals stay cool in summer?

bison shedding fur

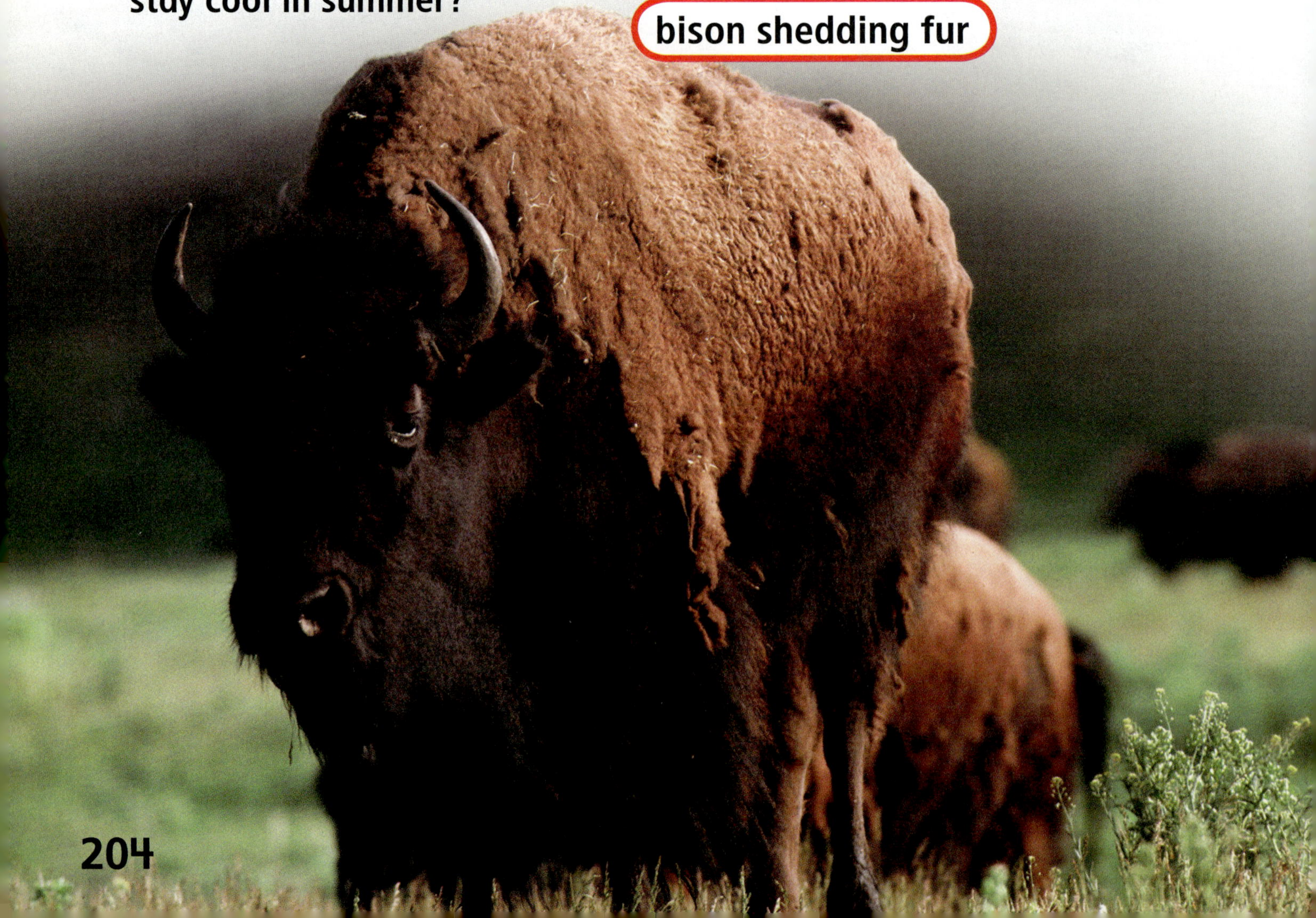

Reading Review

1. **MAIN IDEA AND DETAILS** Copy and complete this chart.

```
                    Summer

                  Main Idea
           Summer is the season after spring.

   detail                detail              detail
The weather can    Some plants grow    Animals have ways
be A _____.       B _____.           to stay C _____.
```

2. **DRAW CONCLUSIONS** Why do some people like cold drinks in summer?

3. **VOCABULARY** Use the word **summer** to tell about the picture.

Test Prep

4. Write about how plants change from spring to summer.

Links

Math

Use a Calendar

Use a calendar to answer these questions. How many months are there? What are their names? Which ones are summer months? When does summer begin? When does it end?

JUNE						
SUN	MON	TUE	WED	THU	FRI	SAT
				1	2	3	4
5	6	7	8	9	10	11
12	13	14	15	16	17	18
19	20	21	22	23	24	25
26	27	28	29	30		

 For more links and activities, go to www.hspscience.com

Lesson 3

What Is Fall?

Fast Fact

Apples get ripe in fall. People pick the apples and make them into foods to eat all year. You can compare fruits in many ways.

Investigate

Compare Seeds

You need

- fruits with seeds

- hand lens

Step 1

Look at the fruits with the hand lens. Find the seeds. **Compare** the seeds. How are they alike? How are they different?

Step 2

Draw and label pictures of the fruits and seeds.

Step 3

Talk about how the seeds are alike. Then talk about how they are different.

Inquiry Skill

Look at the sizes, shapes, and colors of the seeds to **compare** them.

Reading in Science

VOCABULARY
fall
migrate

 READING FOCUS SKILL
CAUSE AND EFFECT Look for reasons that plants and animals change in fall.

Fall

Fall is the season after summer. It has fewer hours of daylight than summer. The temperature gets cooler. People wear heavier clothes.

 CAUSE AND EFFECT Why do people wear heavier clothes in fall?

How can you tell it is fall?

cleaning up leaves

Plants in Fall

In many places, leaves change color and fall from the trees. This happens because they do not get as much daylight as in summer.

Some fruits get ripe in fall. Then they are ready to pick and eat.

Focus Skill **CAUSE AND EFFECT** **Why do we pick some fruits in fall?**

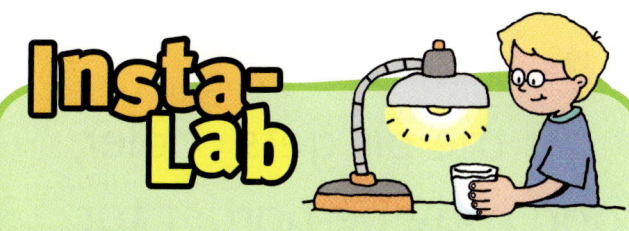

Insta-Lab

Swim!

Why do you swim in summer and not in fall? Put a cup of water under a lamp. **CAUTION:** The lamp may be hot! Put another cup of water in a shady place. Which cup of water warms up faster?

squashes

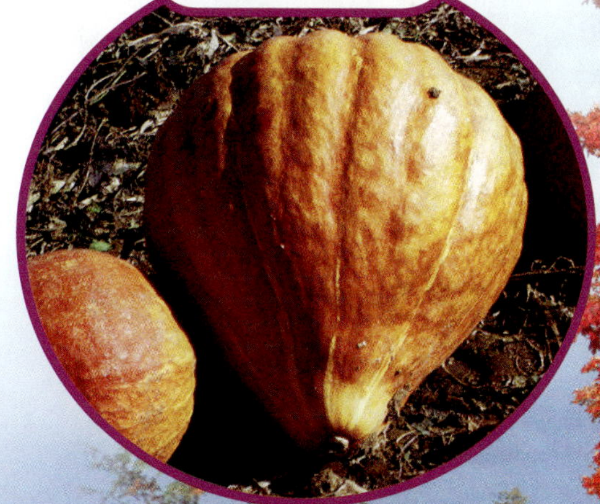

maple trees

Animals in Fall

As the air gets cooler, food may be harder for animals to find. Some animals store food to eat later. Others **migrate**, or move to new places, to find food.

squirrel carrying food

CAUSE AND EFFECT
Why do some animals store food in fall?

geese migrating

Reading Review

1. **CAUSE AND EFFECT** Copy and complete this chart.

Fall

cause | effect

Weather gets **A** _____ in fall. → People wear **B** _____ clothes.

There is not as much **C** _____. → Some trees lose their **D** _____.

There is not as much food for **E** _____. → Some animals **F** _____ food for later.

2. **SUMMARIZE** Use the chart to summarize what happens in fall.

3. **VOCABULARY** Use the word **fall** to tell about these plants.

Test Prep

4. Why do some animals move to new places in fall?
   A. to stay cool
   B. to find food
   C. to grow seeds
   D. to have their young

Links

Writing

Apple Book

Work with a partner to draw healthful snacks that are made with apples. Write a sentence for each picture. Bind the pictures together to make a book.

 For more links and activities, go to www.hspscience.com

211

Lesson 4

What Is Winter?

Fast Fact

Some trees stay green all year, even in winter. Draw a conclusion about what happens to plants and animals in winter.

Investigate

How to Stay Warm

You need

- plastic bag
- ice water
- mitten

Step 1

Put your hand in the bag. Dip the bag into the water. How does your hand feel?

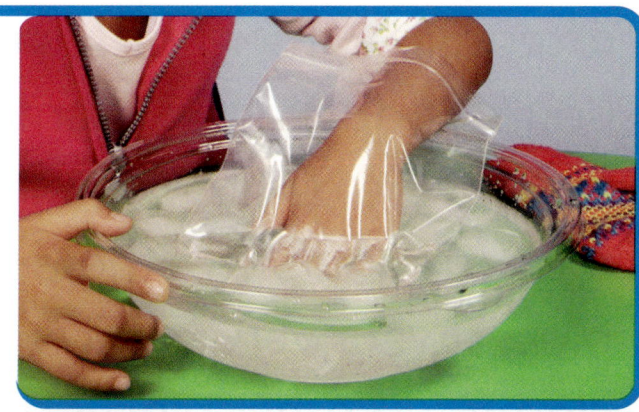

Step 2

Put on the mitten. Put your hand in the bag, and dip the bag into the water. How does your hand feel?

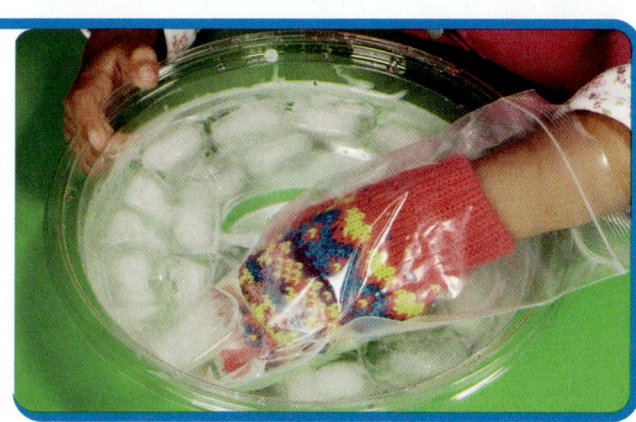

Step 3

Draw a conclusion about what can keep you warm in winter.

Inquiry Skill

To **draw a conclusion**, use what you observed to decide what something means.

213

Reading in Science

VOCABULARY
winter

 READING FOCUS SKILL
MAIN IDEA AND DETAILS Look for the main ideas about winter.

Winter

Winter is the season after fall. Winter has fewer hours of daylight. In some places, the air is cold. Snow may fall. People in these places wear very heavy clothes. In other places, the air may just get cooler.

How can you tell it is winter?

MAIN IDEA AND DETAILS How is winter different from fall?

214

Plants in Winter

Many plants have no leaves in winter. Other plants stay green.

Some plants rest. They do not grow until it gets warm again. Other plants die.

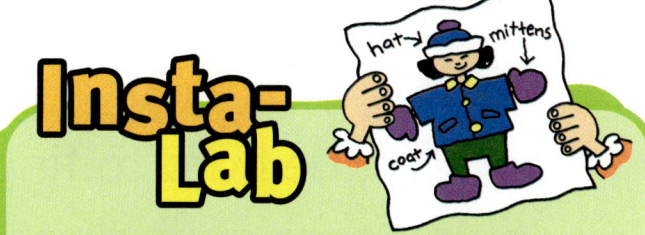

Insta-Lab

Cold-Weather Clothes

Draw a picture of yourself in very cold weather. Label each thing you wear to stay warm. Then show your work to a partner. Tell how each piece of clothing keeps you warm.

Focus Skill **MAIN IDEA AND DETAILS**

What can happen to plants in the winter?

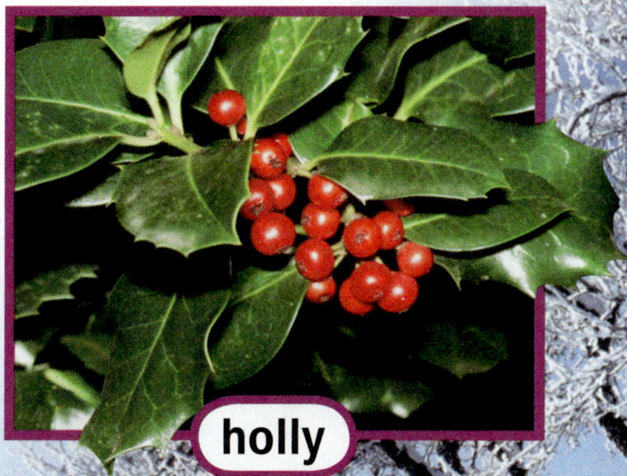

holly

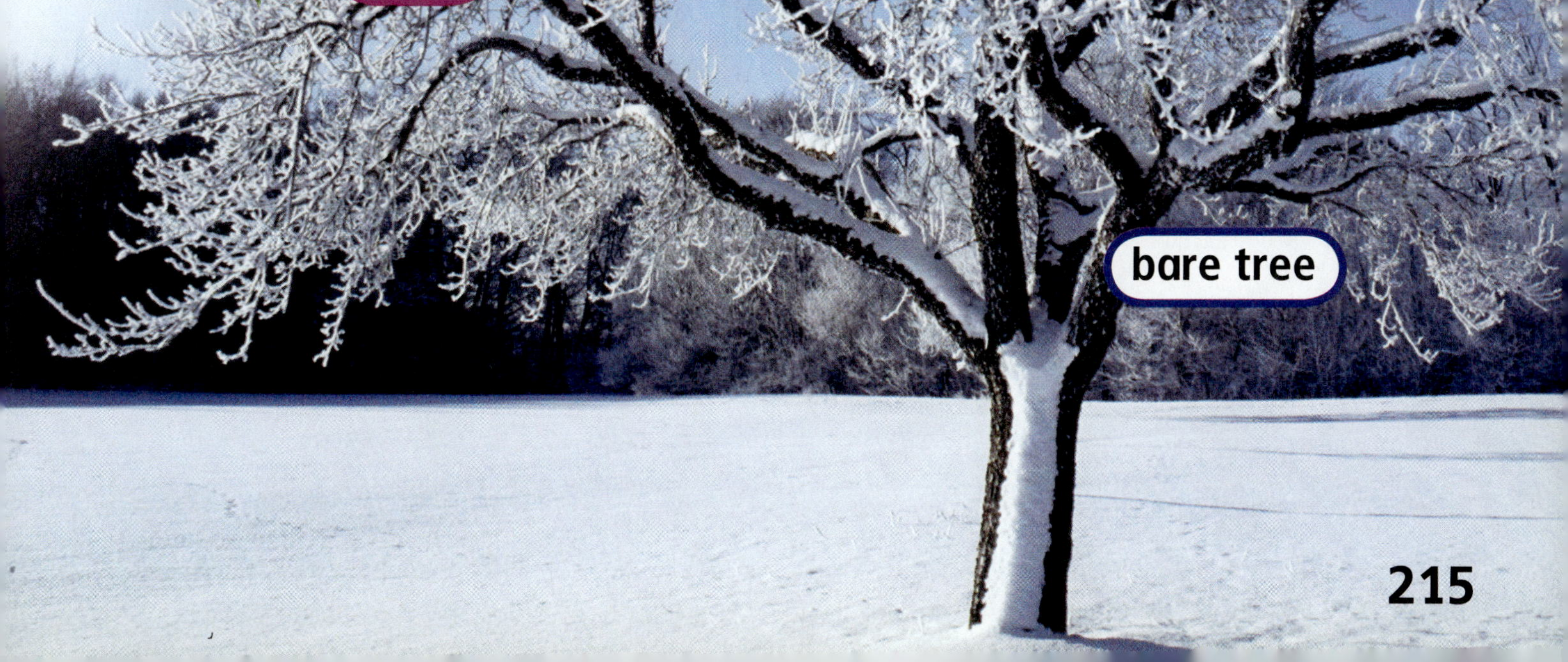

bare tree

Animals in Winter

Food can be hard to find in winter. Some animals eat food that they stored in fall. Others sleep until spring.

Some animals change color to stay safe. Some grow thick coats to stay warm.

MAIN IDEA AND DETAILS How do some animals change in winter?

This animal changes color in winter.

This animal grows a thick coat in winter.

Reading Review

1. **MAIN IDEA AND DETAILS** Copy and complete this chart.

   Winter

   Main Idea
   Winter is the season after fall.

detail	detail	detail	detail
The weather may get **A** _____.	In some places, **B** _____ falls.	Plants may rest or **C** _____.	Some animals grow thick **D** _____ to stay warm.

2. **DRAW CONCLUSIONS** Why do you think it is hard for animals to find food in winter?

3. **VOCABULARY** Tell how you know this picture shows winter.

Test Prep

4. How can winter be different in different places?

Links

Social Studies

Snowy Places

Look at a map of the United States. Find places in the United States where it snows in winter. Where are these places? Make a list. Tell how the places are alike.

 For more links and activities, go to www.hspscience.com

Snow Is Useful

When snow falls, it is soft and fluffy. Over time, it gets packed down.

Snow is strong and holds heat well. Some people use it to build homes. These homes are called igloos.

The Inuit

Canada is a country north of the United States. In Canada, there is a group of people called Inuit. Sometimes the Inuit have to travel during the winter. They move across large areas of snow and ice.

Flaky Facts

To use a tent on the snow and ice would be too cold. So the Inuit use snow to build an igloo.

The Inuit cut snow into blocks. Then they stack the blocks into a curved shape. It looks sort of like the top of your head. A narrow tunnel is built. It is used to get into the igloo. The tunnel stops the wind from blowing in.

- The largest snowflake was more than a foot across.
- No two snowflakes are alike.
- All snowflakes have six sides.
- Stampede Pass, Washington, is the snow capital of the United States!

THINK ABOUT IT

Why do you think igloos are built only during the winter?

Find out more! Log on to www.hspscience.com

219

Meet Ivy the Inventor

During the fall and winter, it gets dark outside earlier. That means things like mailboxes may be hard to see. Ivy Lumpkin came up with an idea to help people see mailboxes better.

Ivy put two nightlights into a clear tube. The lights run on batteries. Then she put a mailbox on top of the tube. When it is dark out, the nightlights shine and people can see the post. Bright idea, Ivy!

SCIENCE Projects
for Home or School
You Can Do It!

Cool Colors

What to Do

1. Put a thermometer inside each T-shirt.
2. Put the T-shirts in a sunny place. Record the temperature in each.
3. Wait one hour. Record the temperatures. Which colors stayed cooler? Which color got the warmest?

Materials
- 3 thermometers
- 3 T-shirts

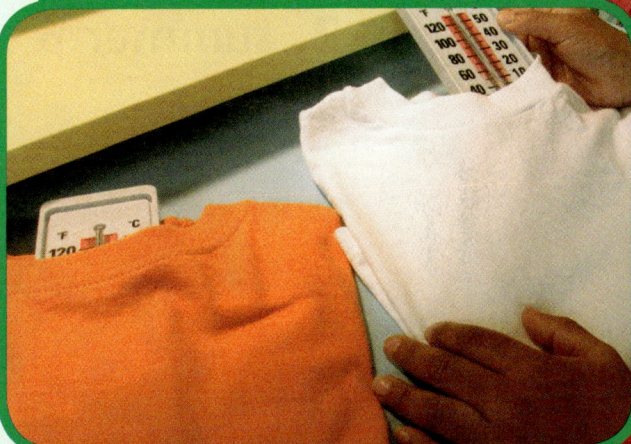

Draw Conclusions
What kinds of colors will help you stay cool?

Favorite Season Graphs

Take a survey. Find out which season your class likes best. Make a bar graph to show what you learn. Share your graph with your classmates.

Chapter 6

Review and Test Preparation

Vocabulary Review

Match the word to its picture.

1. **spring** p. 196
2. **summer** p. 202
3. **fall** p. 208
4. **winter** p. 214

A.

B.

C.

D.

Check Understanding

5. What is a season? Tell **details** about one season.

6. In which season would you see trees with many green leaves? Tell why.

7. Why do some animals shed some of their fur in summer?
   A. to stay warm
   B. to hide
   C. to find food
   D. to stay cool

Critical Thinking

8. Tell how the tree changes with each season.

Chapter

7 Objects in the Sky

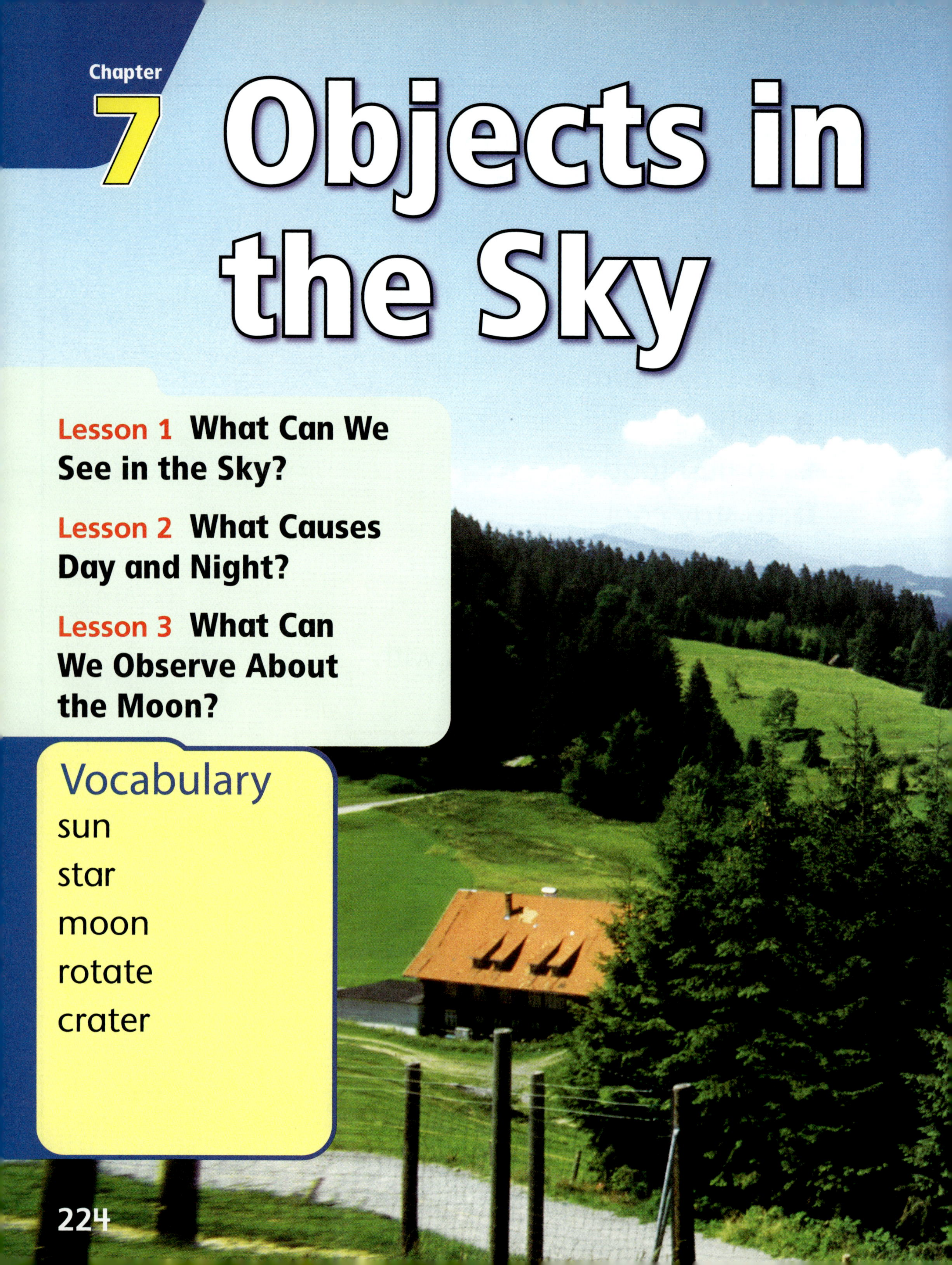

Lesson 1 What Can We See in the Sky?

Lesson 2 What Causes Day and Night?

Lesson 3 What Can We Observe About the Moon?

Vocabulary
sun
star
moon
rotate
crater

I wonder...
Why can you sometimes see the moon in the daytime?
What do you wonder?

Lesson 1

What Can We See in the Sky?

Fast Fact

Moving air causes some of the light from the stars to bend. This makes the stars seem to twinkle. You can communicate about what you see in the sky.

Investigate

The Daytime Sky

You need

- colored paper

- crayons

Step 1

Look out the window. Observe the daytime sky.

Step 2

Draw pictures of what you see. Write about it.

Step 3

Share your work with a partner. Use it to help you **communicate** what you observed.

Inquiry Skill

You can use writing and pictures to help you **communicate**.

Reading in Science

VOCABULARY
sun
star
moon

 READING FOCUS SKILL

COMPARE AND CONTRAST Look for ways the daytime and nighttime skies are alike and ways they are different.

Observing the Sky

In the daytime sky, you may see clouds and the sun. The **sun** is the star closest to Earth. A **star** is an object in the sky that gives off its own light. The sun lights Earth in the daytime.

sun

228

In the nighttime sky, you may see stars, planets, and the moon. The **moon** is a huge ball of rock. It does not give off its own light. Its light comes from the sun.

moon

COMPARE AND CONTRAST How are the daytime sky and the nighttime sky different?

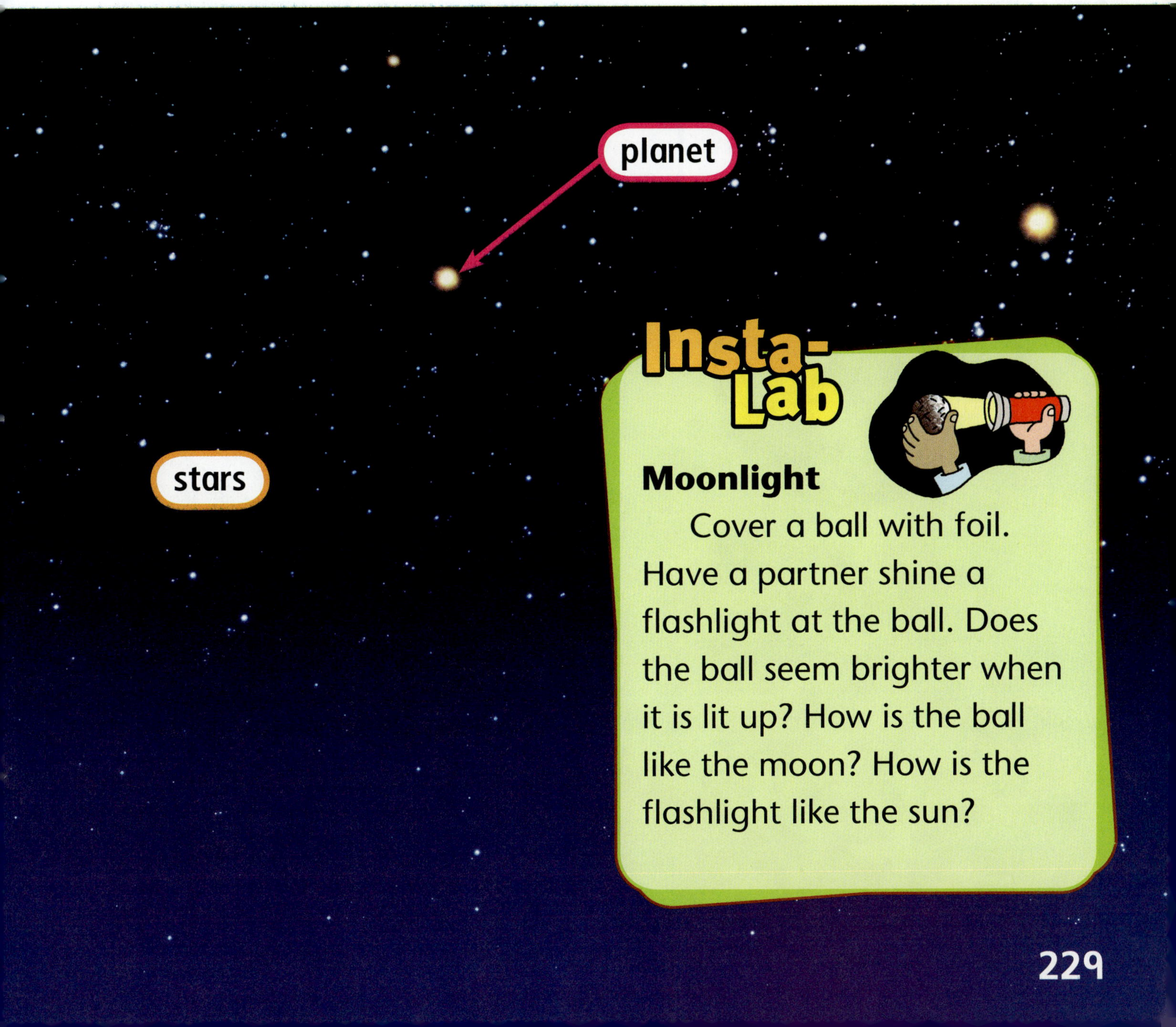

planet

stars

Insta-Lab

Moonlight
Cover a ball with foil. Have a partner shine a flashlight at the ball. Does the ball seem brighter when it is lit up? How is the ball like the moon? How is the flashlight like the sun?

229

Science Up Close

Telescopes

You can look at the sky with a telescope. A telescope is a tool that makes things that are far away look closer. It can help you see more of the moon, stars, and planets.

Look at the planet Mars with just your eyes. This is what you see.

Look at Mars with a telescope. This is what you see. How much more can you see now?

For more links and activities, go to www.hspscience.com

Reading Review

1. **COMPARE AND CONTRAST** Copy and complete this chart.

   alike
   - In the daytime and nighttime sky, you can sometimes see clouds and the moon.

   different
   - In the daytime sky, you may see A _____ and the sun.
   - In the nighttime sky, you may see B _____, planets, and the moon.
   - In the daytime, the C _____ gives off light.
   - In the nighttime, the stars give off light, but the D _____ does not.

2. **DRAW CONCLUSIONS** Why do you think the sun is much brighter than the moon?

3. **VOCABULARY** Use the words **sun** and **star** to talk about this picture.

Test Prep

4. What does a telescope do?
   - **A.** It makes things that are far away look closer.
   - **B.** It makes things that are close look farther away.
   - **C.** It makes very big things look farther away.
   - **D.** It makes very big things look smaller.

Links

Writing

Stories About the Sky

Long ago, people made up stories about what they saw in the sky. Write your own story about something in the sky. Then draw a picture for your story.

The sun is a happy teacher. The clouds are her students.

For more links and activities, go to www.hspscience.com

Lesson 2

What Causes Day and Night?

Fast Fact

When it is daytime in the United States, it is nighttime in China. You can make a model to see why this happens.

Investigate

Model Day and Night

You need

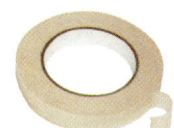
- labels

- tape

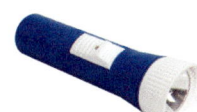
- globe

- flashlight

Step 1

Label the globe Earth. Label the flashlight sun. Use them to **make a model** of Earth and the sun.

Step 2

Make the room dark. Have a partner hold the globe. Shine the flashlight on it.

Step 3

How does the **model** help you see why Earth has day and night?

Inquiry Skill

Make a model to help you see why something happens.

233

Reading in Science

VOCABULARY
rotate

READING FOCUS SKILL
CAUSE AND EFFECT Look for what causes day and night.

Day and Night

Each day, the sun seems to move across the sky. It is not the sun that is moving. It is Earth! Earth rotates. To **rotate** is to spin like a top.

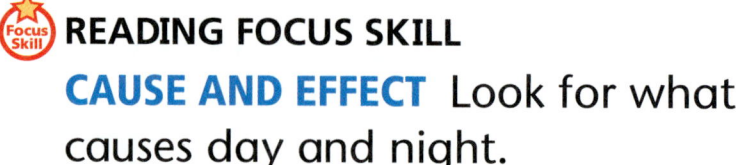

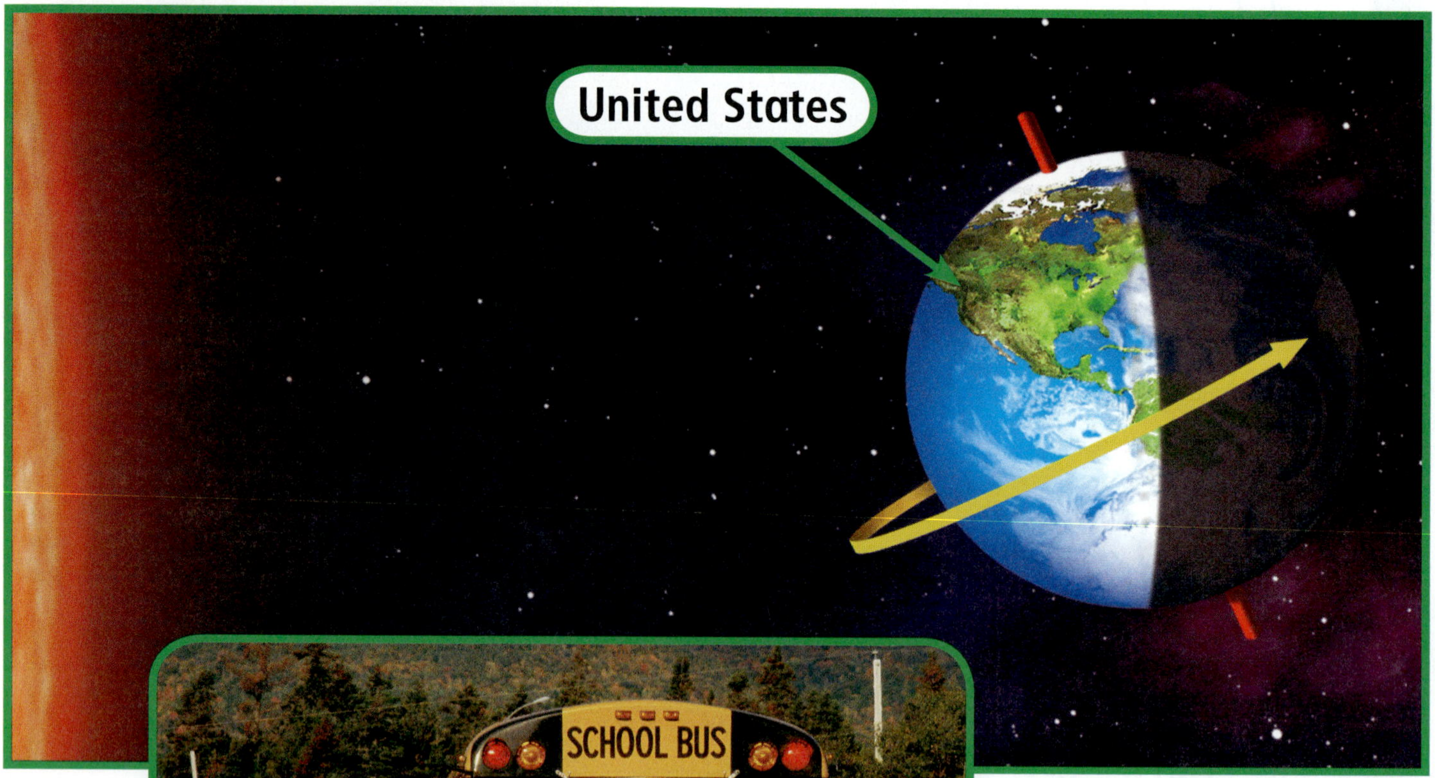

United States

day

As Earth rotates, the side we live on turns toward the sun. The sun lights the sky, and we have day. As Earth keeps rotating, our side turns away from the sun. The sky gets dark, and we have night.

★ **CAUSE AND EFFECT** What do we have when the side of Earth we live on turns toward the sun? Why?

United States

night

Objects in the Sky Seem to Move

The sun, moon, and stars seem to move in the sky. As Earth spins, we turn toward and away from the sun, moon, and stars. We can not feel that we are moving, so it seems to us as if they are.

Insta-Lab

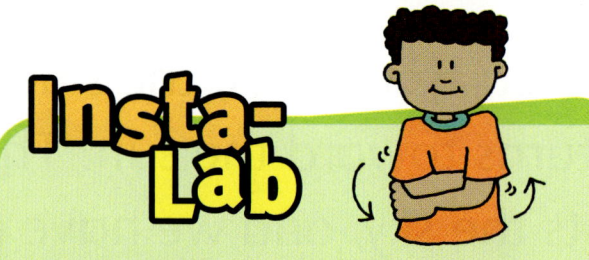

Things Seem to Move

Stand in an open space. Turn around in circles. Do the things around you seem to move? How is this like the way the sun and stars seem to move around Earth?

Focus Skill **CAUSE AND EFFECT** **Why does the sun seem to move in the sky?**

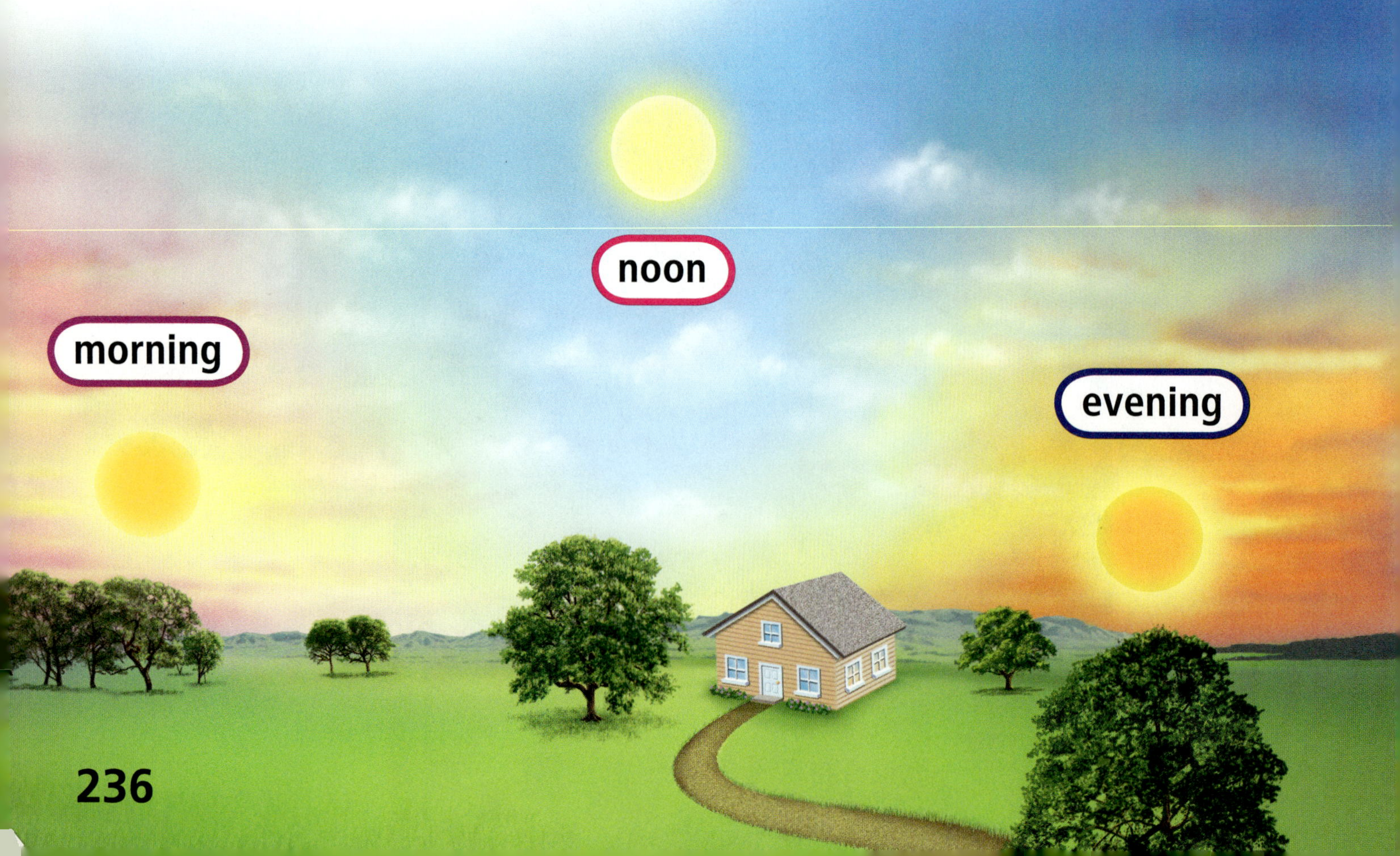
noon
morning
evening

Reading Review

 1. CAUSE AND EFFECT Copy and complete this chart.

Day and Night

cause

As Earth **A** _____, the side we live on turns toward the sun.

The side we live on turns away from the **D** _____.

effect

The **B** _____ lights the sky, and we have **C** _____.

We have **E** _____.

2. SUMMARIZE Use the chart to write a summary of the lesson.

3. VOCABULARY Use the word **rotate** to talk about this picture.

Test Prep

4. Why do we have daytime when China has nighttime?

Links

Math

Time and the Sun

Observe the sun at 8:00 A.M., noon, and 7:00 P.M. Draw and write about what you observe. Then make a prediction. Will the sun be in about the same places at the same times tomorrow? Tell why. Check tomorrow to see if you were right.

 For more links and activities, go to www.hspscience.com

Lesson 3

What Can We Observe About the Moon?

Fast Fact

Much of the moon is covered with dust. It has many craters. You can use what you know to infer how the craters were made.

Investigate

The Surface of the Moon

You need

 • pan of sand

 • spray bottle of water

 • marbles

Step 1

Spray the sand lightly with water.

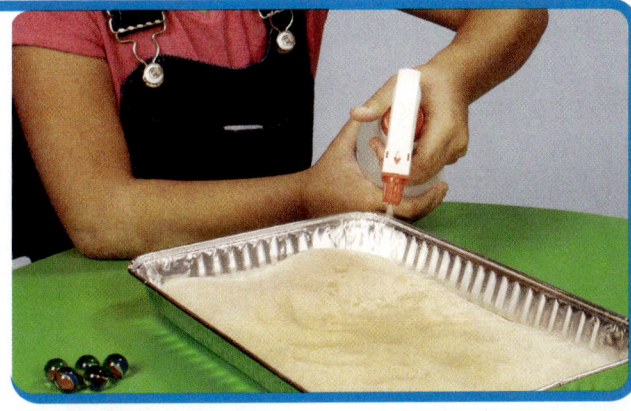

Step 2

Hold the marbles above the sand. Drop them one at a time. Observe.

Step 3

Infer how the moon's craters were made. Compare your ideas with others' ideas.

Inquiry Skill

To **infer**, first observe. Then think about what you see.

Reading in Science

VOCABULARY
crater

 READING FOCUS SKILL
SEQUENCE Look for the order in which the moon seems to change.

Changes in the Moon's Shape

The shape of the moon seems to change a little each night. The changes make a pattern that takes about 29 days.

On some nights, you can not see the moon at all. Then you start to see a little of it. After about 15 days, you see the moon as a full circle. Then you see less of it each night. In about 14 more days, you can not see it again.

Day 22
quarter moon

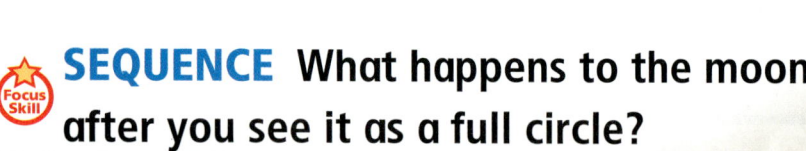 **SEQUENCE** What happens to the moon after you see it as a full circle?

240

Moon Changes

The picture cards show how the moon looks. Put them in order. Start with the new moon. Then use the pictures to tell about how the moon seems to change.

Day 1
new moon

Day 8
quarter moon

Day 15
full moon

Exploring the Moon

In 1969, astronauts landed on the moon for the first time. First, they saw the moon's gray dust and craters. A **crater** is a hole that is shaped like a bowl in a surface. Next, the astronauts explored the moon. Later, they brought moon rocks back to Earth.

SEQUENCE What did the astronauts do after they landed on the moon?

astronaut on the moon

footprints in moon dust

moon rock

Reading Review

1. **SEQUENCE** Copy and complete this chart.

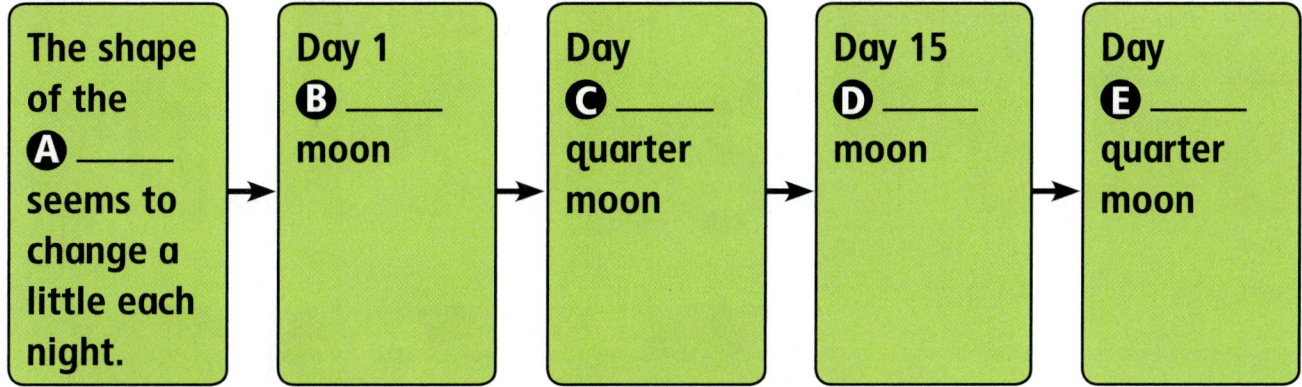

| The shape of the A _____ seems to change a little each night. | Day 1 B _____ moon | Day C _____ quarter moon | Day 15 D _____ moon | Day E _____ quarter moon |

2. **SUMMARIZE** Write sentences to summarize this lesson.

3. **VOCABULARY** Use the word **crater** to talk about this picture.

Test Prep

4. How many days is it from one new moon to the next new moon?
   A. 8
   B. 15
   C. 22
   D. 29

Links

Writing

Writing About the Moon
Research what the moon is like. Then write sentences about exploring the moon yourself. What would you do there? What would you want to find out? Draw pictures to go with your sentences.

I would walk in the craters.

 For more links and activities, go to www.hspscience.com

Smart Spacesuits

Right now, people are living and working on the space station. The people are called astronauts.

Spacesuits have to protect astronauts from the cold. The suits also have to let astronauts move their arms and hands. That is so the astronauts can add parts or do repairs.

Breathtaking Fact

When astronauts go outside, they wear special spacesuits. That is because it is very cold in space and there is no air to breathe.

Scientists have made the spacesuits better. They added a computer that is sewn into the suit. The computer will help astronauts do their work.

Scientists also made the gloves better. Now, the fingers and thumbs are much easier to move. The gloves are also heated to help the astronauts work outside longer.

THINK ABOUT IT
Why do you think astronauts have to wear special suits?

Find out more! Log on to www.hspscience.com

Studying Mars

Joy Crisp loves rocks and volcanoes. Now she is studying rocks and volcanoes on Mars. Mars is a planet in space.

Crisp uses machines on Earth to watch two robot rovers on Mars. The rovers are like little radio controlled trucks. They use special tools to study rocks and dirt.

Scientists are looking to find if Mars ever had water. If so, scientists say people might someday live on Mars.

SCIENCE Projects for Home or School
You Can Do It!

Warm or Cool

What to Do

1. When is it warmest outside? Make a chart. Predict what you will find out.
2. Use a thermometer. Find the temperature at three different times of day.
3. Write the temperatures in the chart. Were your predictions correct?

Materials
- thermometer

Draw Conclusions
Why is the temperature different at different times of day? What does the sun do to Earth?

Moon Journal

Keep a moon journal. Go outside with a family member each night for one month. Find the moon. Draw what you observe. Write the date on each picture. After one month, bind your drawings into a book. Share it with the class.

 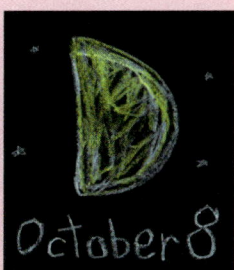

Chapter 7

Review and Test Preparation

Vocabulary Review

Choose the best word to complete each sentence.

sun p. 228   **rotate** p. 234
moon p. 229   **crater** p. 242

1. A word that means spin is ___.

2. A ball of rock whose light comes from the sun is the ___.

3. The star closest to Earth is the ___.

4. A hole in the surface of the moon that is shaped like a bowl is a ___.

Check Understanding

5. Explain the **effect** when our side of Earth turns toward the sun. Use this picture to help you.

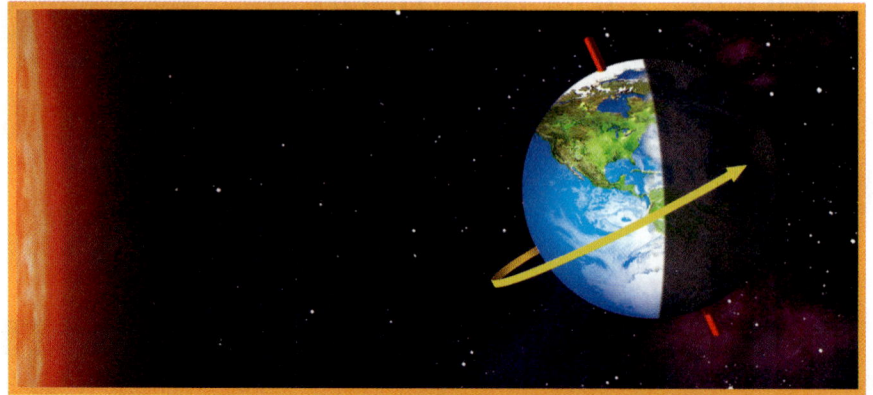

6. Which object in the sky gives off its own light?

   A. cloud   **C.** moon

   B. Earth   **D.** star

7. Each photo is part of a **sequence**. Which one shows the moon eight days after a new moon?

F.    **H.**

G.    **J.**

Critical Thinking

8. Juan looks at the sky and sees what this picture shows. Tell what you know about each object he sees.

249

References

Contents

Health Handbook

Your Senses	R1
Your Skeletal System	R4
Your Muscular System	R5
Your Nervous System	R6
Your Digestive System	R7
Your Respiratory System	R8
Your Circulatory System	R9
Staying Healthy	R10
Keeping Clean	R11
Caring for Your Teeth	R12

Reading in Science Handbook

Identify the Main Idea and Details	R14
Compare and Contrast	R15
Cause and Effect	R16
Sequence	R17
Draw Conclusions	R18
Summarize	R19

Math in Science Handbook — R20

Safety in Science R26
Glossary R27
Index R45

Health Handbook

Your Senses

You have five senses that tell you about the world. Your five senses are sight, hearing, smell, taste, and touch.

Your Eyes

If you look at your eyes in a mirror, you will see an outer white part, a colored part called the iris, and a dark hole in the middle. This hole is called the pupil.

Caring for Your Eyes

- Have a doctor check your eyes to find out if they are healthy.
- Never look directly at the sun or at very bright lights.
- Wear sunglasses outdoors in bright sunlight and on snow and water.
- Don't touch or rub your eyes.
- Protect your eyes when you play sports.

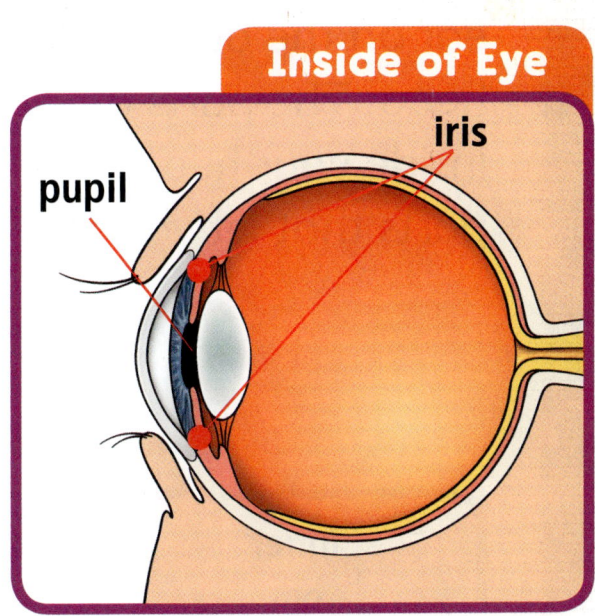

Inside of Eye

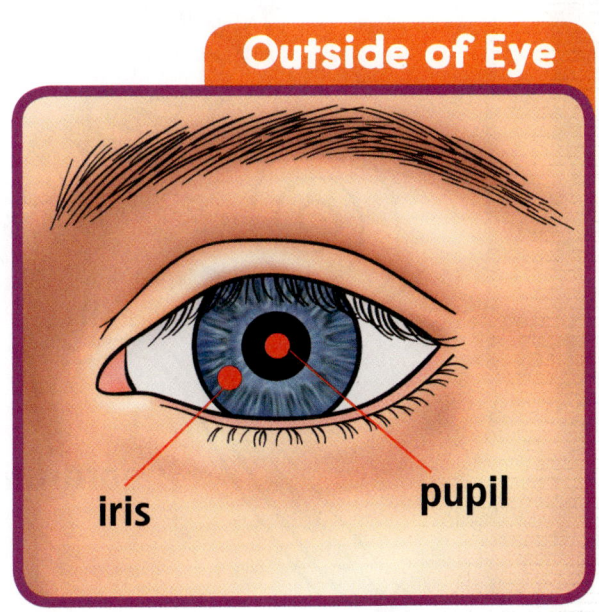

Outside of Eye

R1

Your Senses

Your Ears

Your ears let you hear the things around you. You can see only a small part of the ear on the outside of your head. The parts of your ear inside your head are the parts that let you hear.

Caring for Your Ears

- Have a doctor check your ears.
- Avoid very loud noises.
- Never put anything in your ears.
- Protect your ears when you play sports.

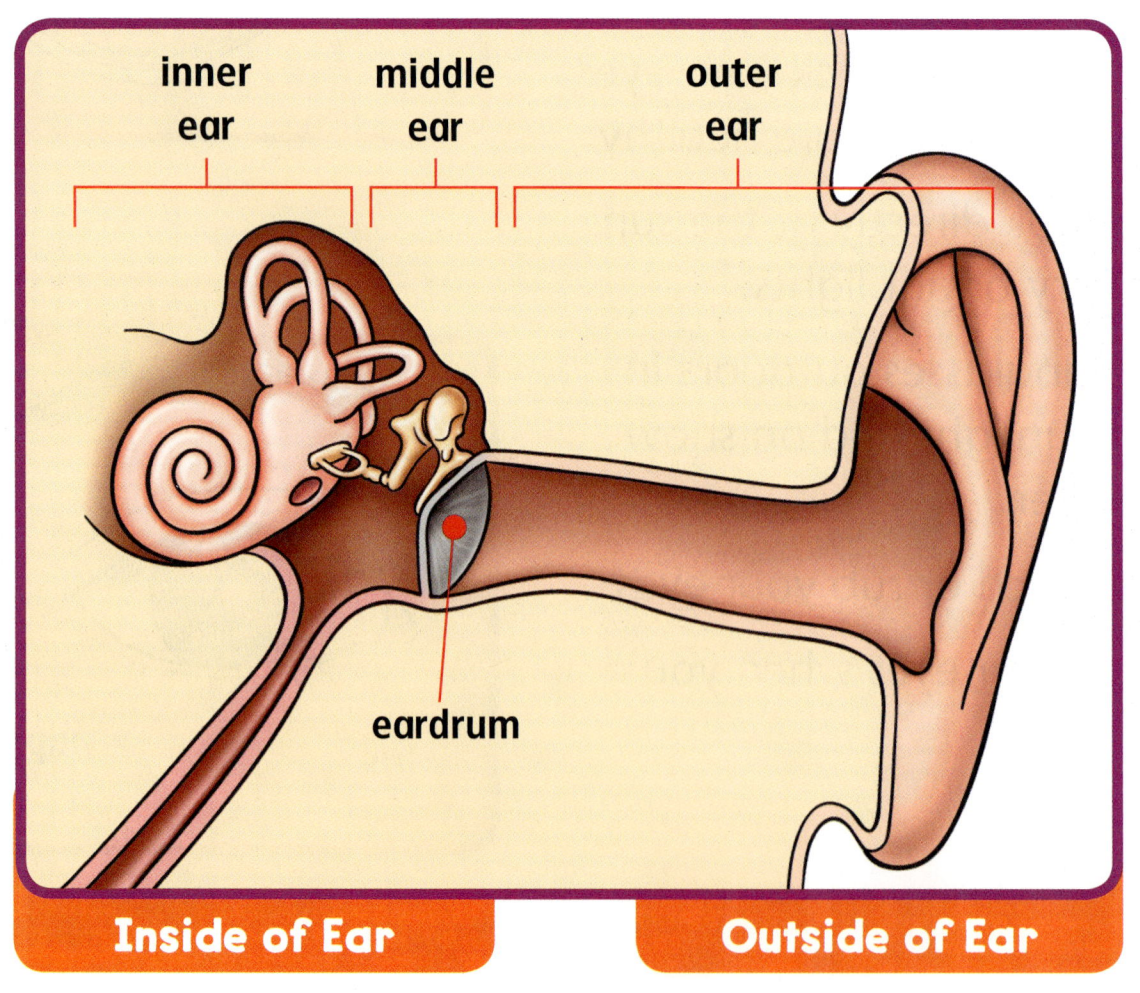

Inside of Ear   **Outside of Ear**

Health Handbook

Your Senses of Smell and Taste

Your nose cleans the air you breathe and lets you smell things. Your nose and tongue help you taste things you eat and drink.

Your Skin

Your skin protects your body from germs. Your skin also gives you your sense of touch.

Caring for Your Skin

- Always wash your hands after coughing or blowing your nose, touching an animal, playing outside, or using the restroom.

- Protect your skin from sunburn. Wear a hat and clothes to cover your skin outdoors.

- Use sunscreen to protect your skin from the sun.

- Wear proper safety pads and a helmet when you play sports, ride a bike, or skate.

Your Skeletal System

Inside your body are many hard, strong bones. They form your skeletal system. The bones in your body protect parts inside your body.

Your skeletal system works with your muscular system to hold your body up and to give it shape.

Caring for Your Skeletal System

- Always wear a helmet and other safety gear when you skate, ride a bike or a scooter, or play sports.
- Eat foods that help keep your bones strong and hard.
- Exercise to help your bones stay strong and healthy.
- Get plenty of rest to help your bones grow.

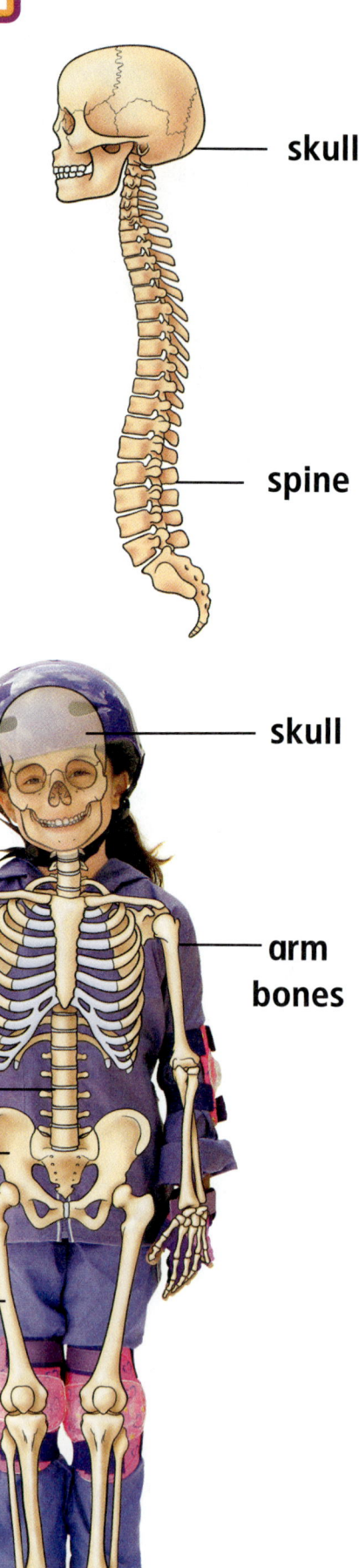

Health Handbook

Your Muscular System

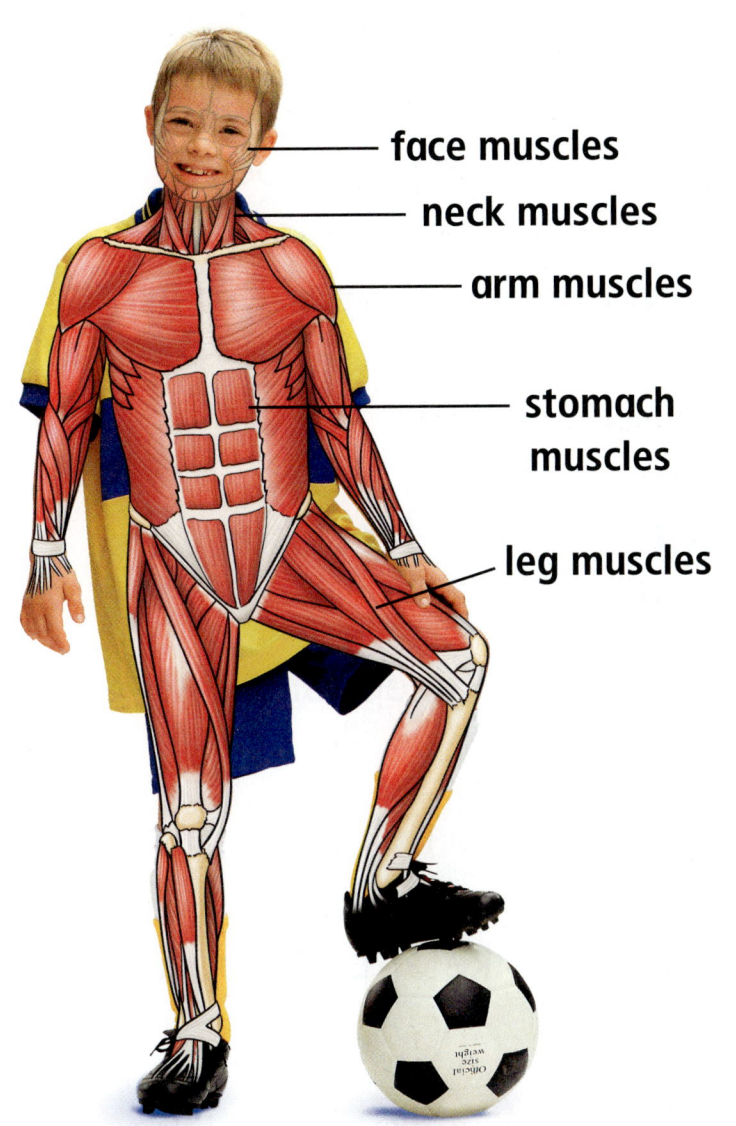

- face muscles
- neck muscles
- arm muscles
- stomach muscles
- leg muscles

Your muscular system is made up of the muscles in your body. Muscles are body parts that help you move.

Caring for Your Muscular System

- Exercise to keep your muscles strong.
- Eat foods that will help your muscles grow.
- Drink plenty of water when you play sports or exercise.
- Rest your muscles after you exercise or play sports.

Your Nervous System

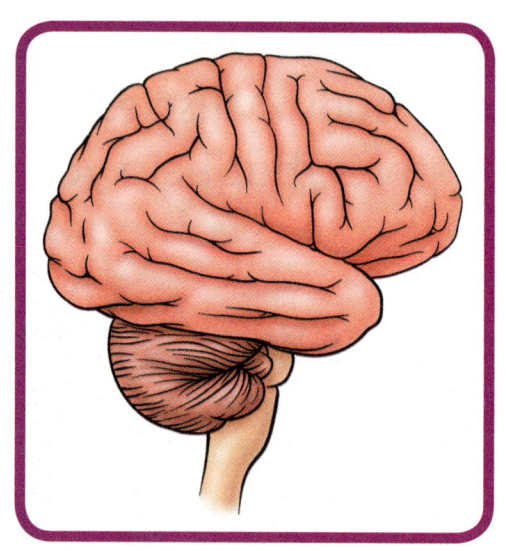

Your brain and your nerves are parts of your nervous system. Your brain keeps your body working. It tells you about the world around you. Your brain also lets you think, remember, and have feelings.

Caring for Your Nervous System

- Get plenty of sleep. Sleeping lets your brain rest.
- Always wear a helmet to protect your head and your brain when you ride a bike or play sports.

Health Handbook

Your Digestive System

Your digestive system helps your body get energy from the foods you eat. Your body needs energy to do things.

When your body digests food, it breaks the food down. Your digestive system keeps the things your body needs. It also gets rid of the things your body does not need to keep.

Caring for Your Digestive System

- Brush and floss your teeth every day.
- Wash your hands before you eat.
- Eat slowly and chew your food well before you swallow.
- Eat vegetables and fruits. They help move foods through your digestive system.

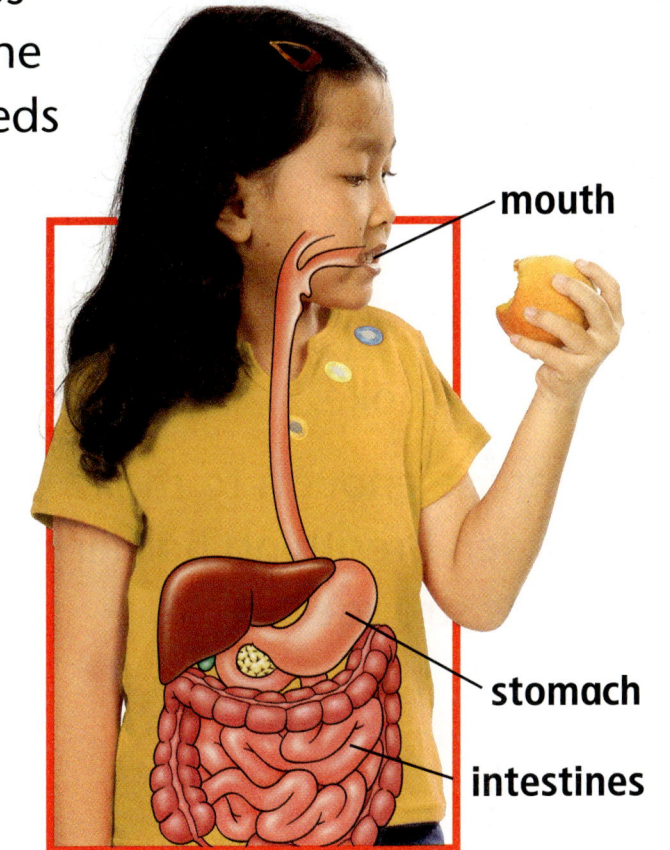

mouth
stomach
intestines

Your Respiratory System

You breathe using your respiratory system. Your mouth, nose, and lungs are all parts of your respiratory system.

Caring for Your Respiratory System

- Never put anything in your nose.
- Never smoke.
- Exercise enough to make you breathe harder. Breathing harder makes your lungs stronger.

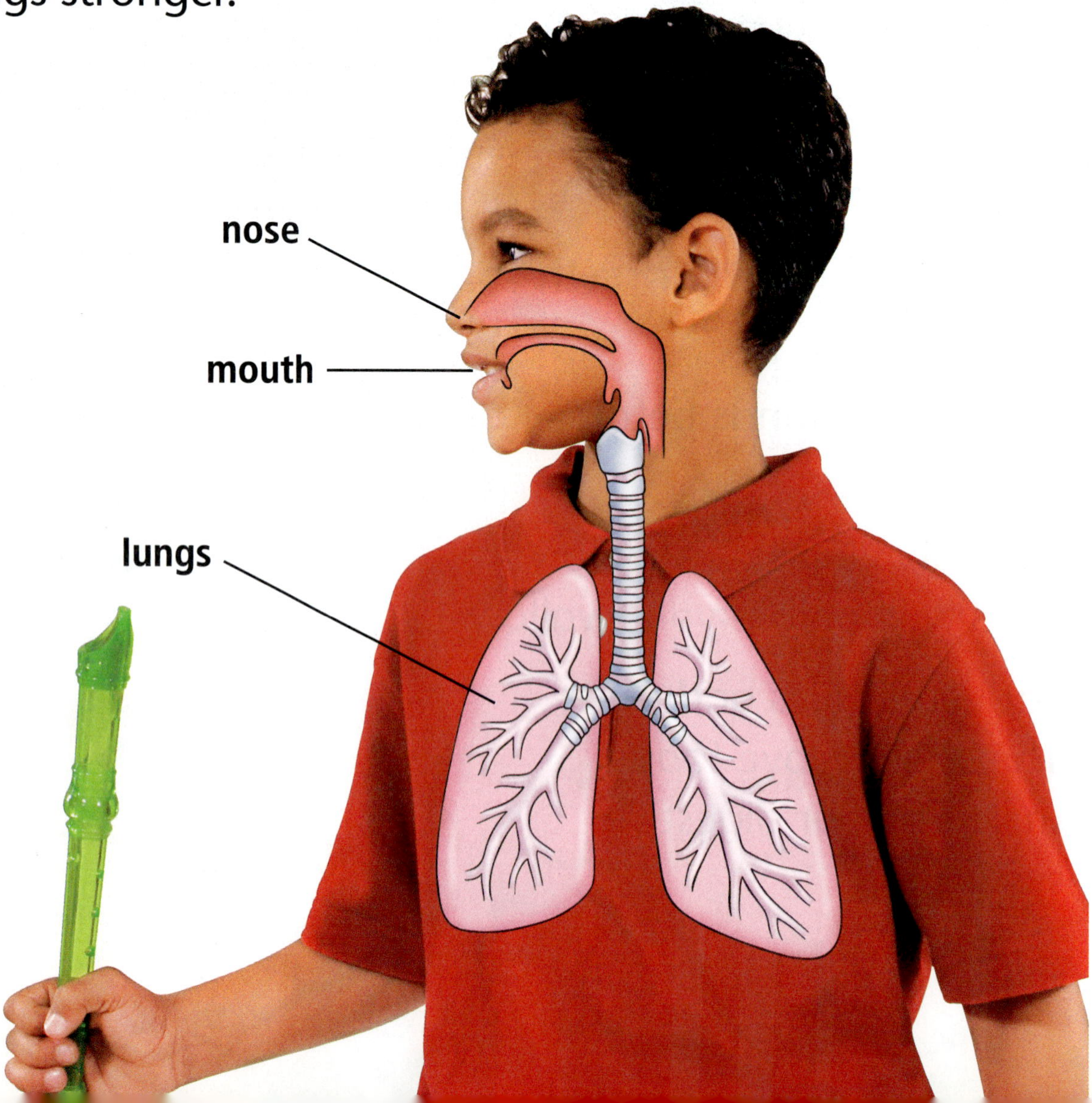

nose

mouth

lungs

Health Handbook

Your Circulatory System

Your circulatory system is made up of your heart and your blood vessels. Your blood carries food energy and oxygen to help your body work. Blood vessels are small tubes. They carry blood from your heart to every part of your body.

Your heart is a muscle. It is beating all the time. As your heart beats, it pumps blood through your blood vessels.

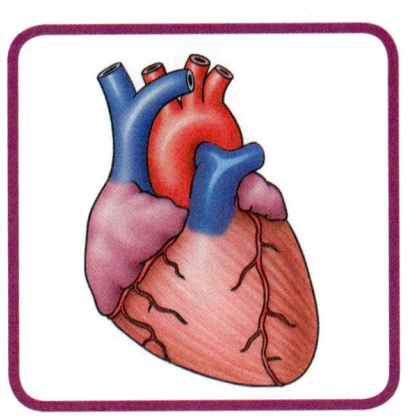

Caring for Your Circulatory System

- Exercise every day to keep your heart strong.
- Eat meats and green leafy vegetables. They help your blood carry oxygen.
- Never touch anyone else's blood.

Staying Healthy

You can do many things to help yourself stay fit and healthy.

You can also avoid doing things that can harm you.

If you know ways to stay safe and healthy and you do these things, you can help yourself have good health.

Getting enough rest

Staying away from alcohol, tobacco, and other drugs

Staying active

Keeping clean

Eating right

Keeping Clean

Health Handbook

Keeping clean helps you stay healthy. You can pick up germs from the things you touch. Washing with soap and water helps remove germs from your skin.

Wash your hands for as long as it takes to say your ABCs. Always wash your hands at these times.

- Before and after you eat
- After coughing or blowing your nose
- After using the restroom
- After touching an animal
- After playing outside

Caring for Your Teeth

Brushing your teeth and gums keeps them clean and healthy. You should brush your teeth at least twice a day. Brush in the morning. Brush before you go to bed at night. It is also good to brush your teeth after you eat if you can.

Health Handbook

Brushing Your Teeth

Use a soft toothbrush that is the right size for you. Always use your own toothbrush. Use only a small amount of toothpaste. It should be about the size of a pea. Be sure to rinse your mouth with water after you brush your teeth.

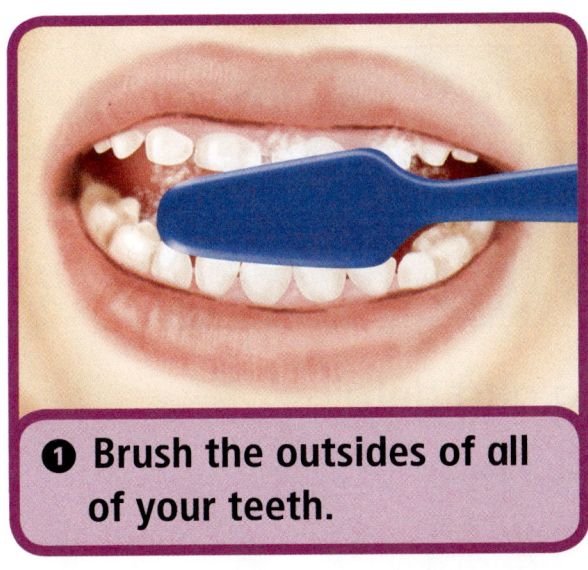
❶ Brush the outsides of all of your teeth.

❷ Brush the insides of all of your teeth.

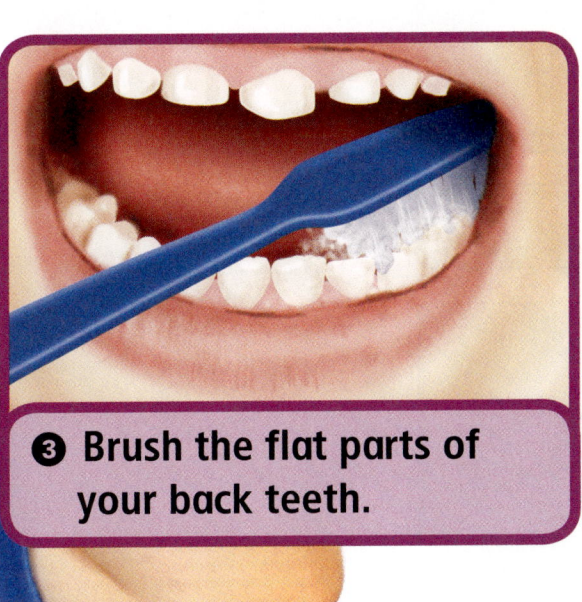
❸ Brush the flat parts of your back teeth.

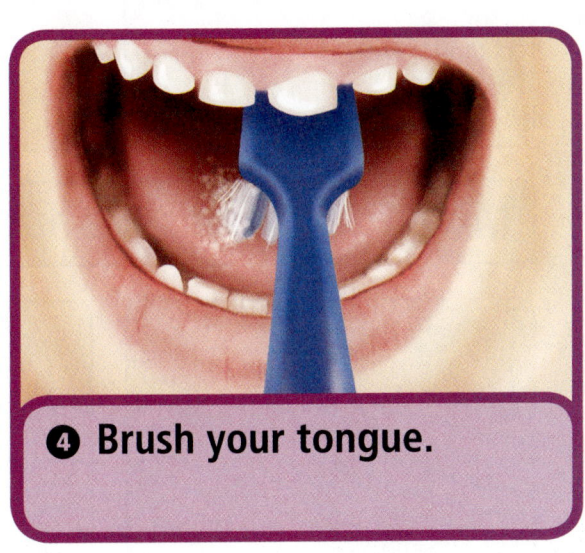
❹ Brush your tongue.

Identify the Main Idea and Details

Some lessons in this science book are written to help you find the main idea. Learning how to find the main idea can help you understand what you read. The main idea of a paragraph is what it is mostly about. The details tell you more about it.

Read this paragraph.

> Lions are hunters. They hunt for meat to eat. Lions can run very fast. They see and hear very well. They need sharp teeth to catch animals. They have sharp teeth to eat the meat they catch.

This chart shows the main idea and details.

Detail: Lions can run very fast.

Detail: Lions see and hear very well.

Main Idea: Lions are hunters.

Detail: Lions hunt for meat to eat.

Detail: Lions have sharp teeth.

Reading in Science Handbook

Compare and Contrast

Some science lessons are written to help you see how things are alike and different. Learning how to compare and contrast can help you understand what you read.

Read this paragraph.

> Birds and mammals are kinds of animals. Birds have a body covering of feathers. Mammals have a body covering of fur. Both birds and mammals need food, air, and water to live. Most birds can fly. Most mammals walk or run.

Here is how you can compare and contrast birds and mammals.

Ways They Are Alike	Ways They Are Different
Compare	**Contrast**
Both are kinds of animals. Both need food, air, and water to live.	Birds have feathers. Mammals have fur. Most birds fly. Most mammals walk or run.

Cause and Effect

Some science lessons are written to help you understand why things happen. You can use a chart like this to help you find cause and effect.

Cause	Effect
A cause is why something happens.	→ An effect is what happens.

Some paragraphs have more than one cause or effect. Read this paragraph.

> Water can be a solid, a liquid, or a gas. When water is very cold it turns into solid ice. When water is heated, it turns into water vapor, a gas.

This chart shows two causes and their effects in the paragraph.

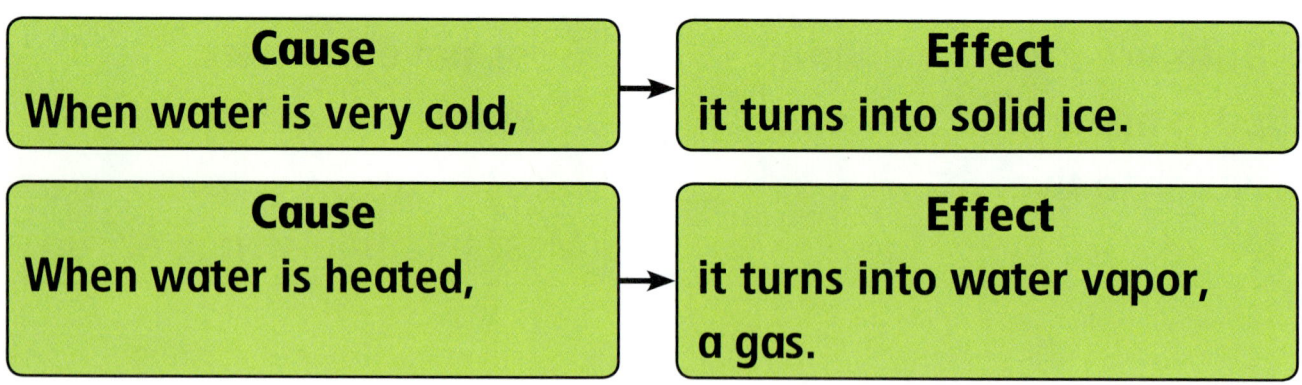

Cause	Effect
When water is very cold,	→ it turns into solid ice.
When water is heated,	→ it turns into water vapor, a gas.

Reading in Science Handbook

Sequence

Learning how to find sequence can help you understand what you read. You can use a chart like this to help you find sequence.

1. The first step. → 2. The next step. → 3. The last step.

Some paragraphs use words that help you understand order. Read this paragraph. Look at the underlined words.

> Each day <u>begins</u> when the sun appears. <u>Then</u> the sun slowly climbs into the sky. At midday, the sun is straight overhead. <u>Then</u> the sun slowly falls back to the horizon. At <u>last</u>, the sun is gone. It is nighttime.

This chart shows the sequence of the paragraph.

1. Day begins when the sun appears. → 2. The sun climbs until midday. → 3. The sun falls back again. It is night.

Draw Conclusions

At the end of some lessons, you will be asked to draw conclusions. When you draw conclusions, you tell what you have learned. What you learned also includes your own ideas.

Read this paragraph.

> Birds use their bills to help them get food. Each kind of bird has its own kind of bill. Birds that eat seeds have strong, short bills. Birds that eat bugs have long, sharp bills. Birds that eat water plants have wide, flat bills.

This chart shows how you can draw conclusions.

What I Read	What I Know	Conclusion:
Birds use their bills to get food. The bills have different shapes.	I have seen ducks up close. They have wide, flat bills.	Ducks are birds that eat water plants.

Reading in Science Handbook

Summarize

At the end of some lessons, you will be asked to summarize what you read. In a summary, some sentences tell the main idea. Some sentences tell details.

Read this paragraph.

> Honey is made by bees. They gather nectar from flowers. Then they fly home to their beehive with the nectar inside special honey stomachs. The bees put the nectar into special honeycomb holes. Then the bees wait. Soon the nectar will change into sweet, sticky honey. The bees cover the holes with wax that they make. They eat some of the honey during the cold winter.

This chart shows how to summarize what the paragraph is about.

Recall Detail
Honey is made by bees.

Recall Detail
Bees gather nectar from flowers.

Recall Detail
The nectar turns into honey in the beehive.

Summary
Bees make honey. They collect nectar from flowers. They bring the nectar to their beehive. The nectar turns to honey in the beehive.

Using Tables, Charts, and Graphs

Gather Data

When you investigate in science, you need to collect data.

Suppose you want to find out what kinds of things are in soil. You can sort the things you find into groups.

Things I Found in One Cup of Soil

Parts of Plants

Small Rocks

Parts of Animals

By studying the circles, you can see the different items found in soil. However, you might display the data in a different way. For example, you could use a tally table.

Math in Science Handbook

Reading a Tally Table

You can show your data in a tally table.

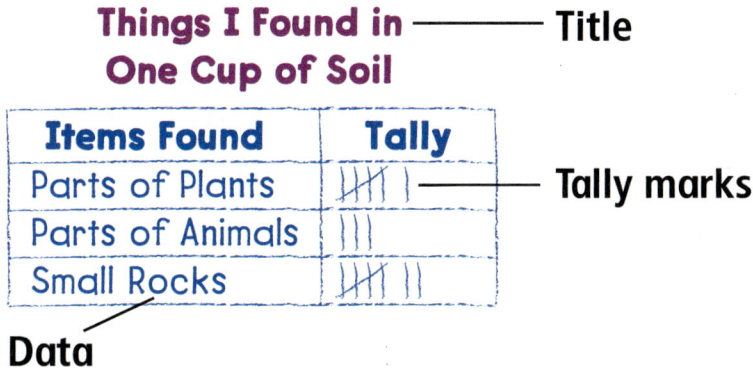

How to Read a Tally Table

1. **Read** the tally table. Use the labels.
2. **Study** the data.
3. **Count** the tally marks.
4. **Draw conclusions**. Ask yourself questions like the ones on this page.

Skills Practice

1. How many parts of plants were found in the soil?
2. How many more small rocks were found in the soil than parts of animals?
3. How many parts of plants and parts of animals were found?

R21

Using Tables, Charts, and Graphs

Reading a Bar Graph

People keep many kinds of animals as pets. This bar graph shows the animal groups pets belong to. A bar graph can be used to compare data.

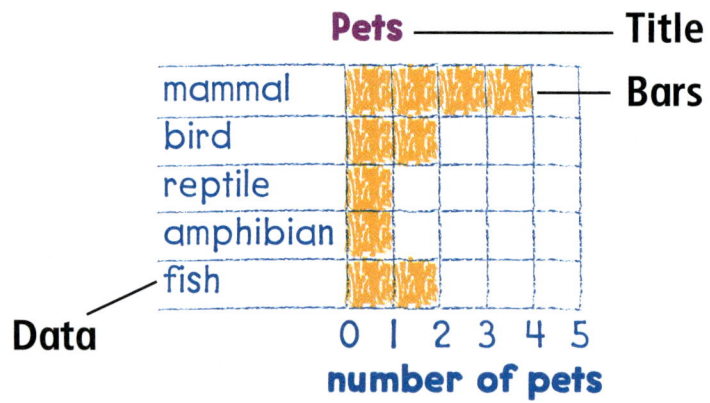

How to Read a Bar Graph

1. **Look** at the title to learn what kind of information is shown.
2. **Read** the graph. Use the labels.
3. **Study** the data. Compare the bars.
4. **Draw conclusions**. Ask yourself questions like the ones on this page.

Skills Practice

1. How many pets are mammals?
2. How many pets are birds?
3. How many more pets are mammals than fish?

Math in Science Handbook

Reading a Pictograph

A second-grade class was asked to choose their favorite season. A pictograph was made to show the results. A pictograph uses pictures to show information.

How to Read a Pictograph

1. **Look** at the title to learn what kind of information is shown.

2. **Read** the graph. Use the labels.

3. **Study** the data. Compare the number of pictures in each row.

4. **Draw conclusions**. Ask yourself questions like the ones on this page.

Skills Practice

1. Which season did the most classmates choose?

2. Which season did the fewest classmates choose?

3. How many classmates in all chose summer or winter?

R23

Measurements

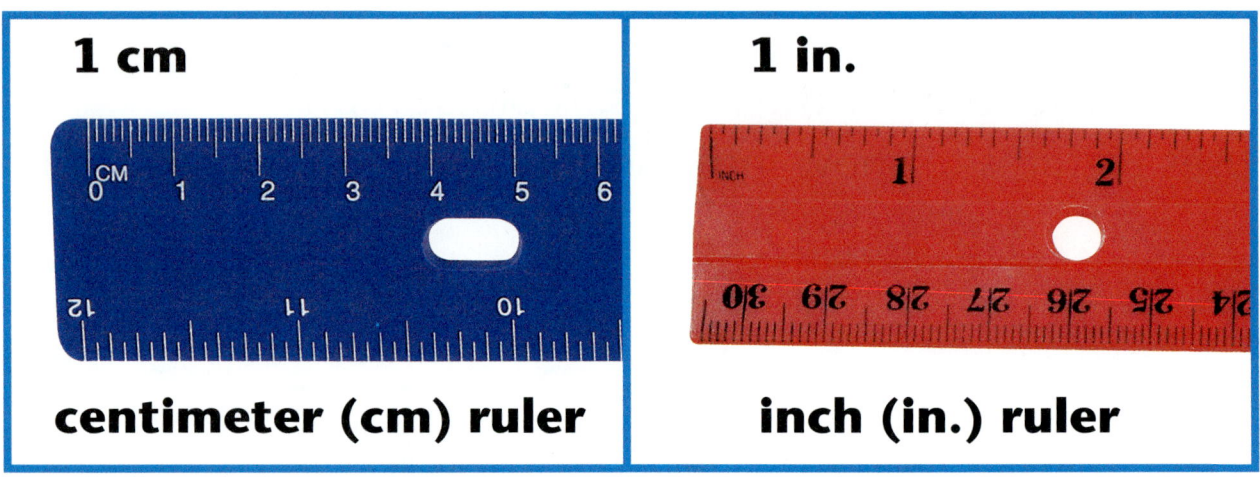

centimeter (cm) ruler

inch (in.) ruler

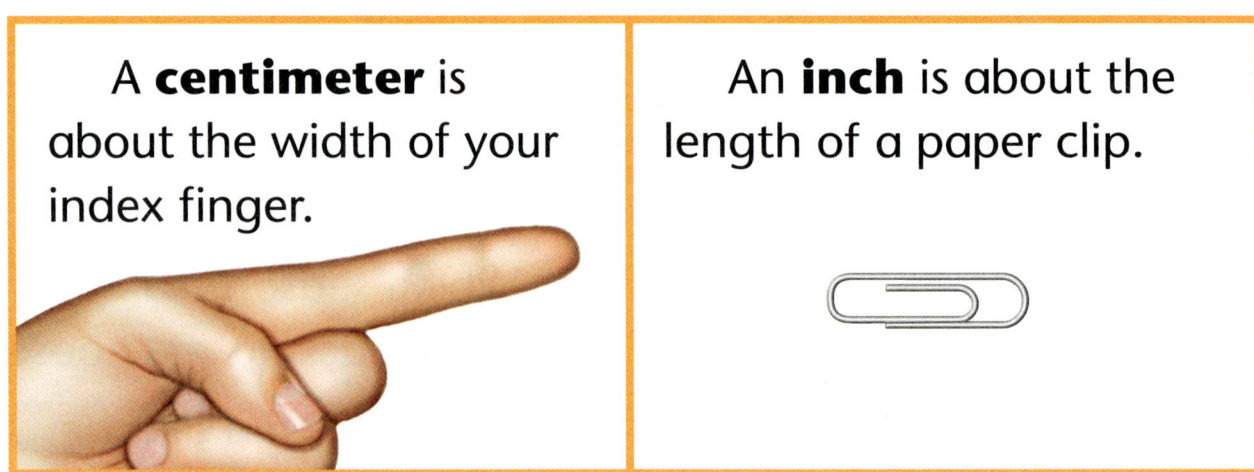

A **centimeter** is about the width of your index finger.

An **inch** is about the length of a paper clip.

Math in Science Handbook

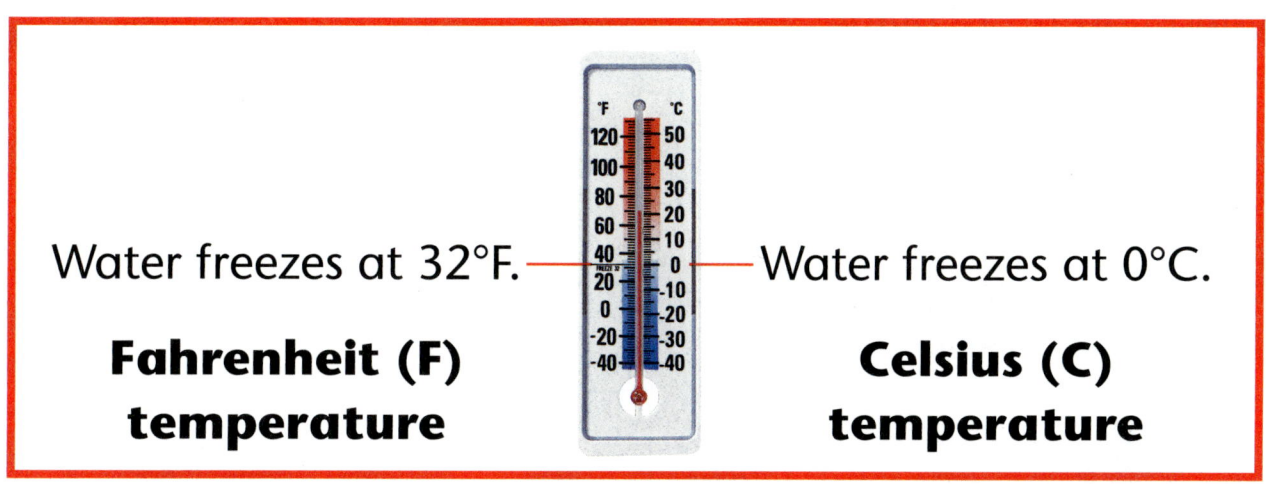

Water freezes at 32°F. — Water freezes at 0°C.

Fahrenheit (F) temperature — **Celsius (C) temperature**

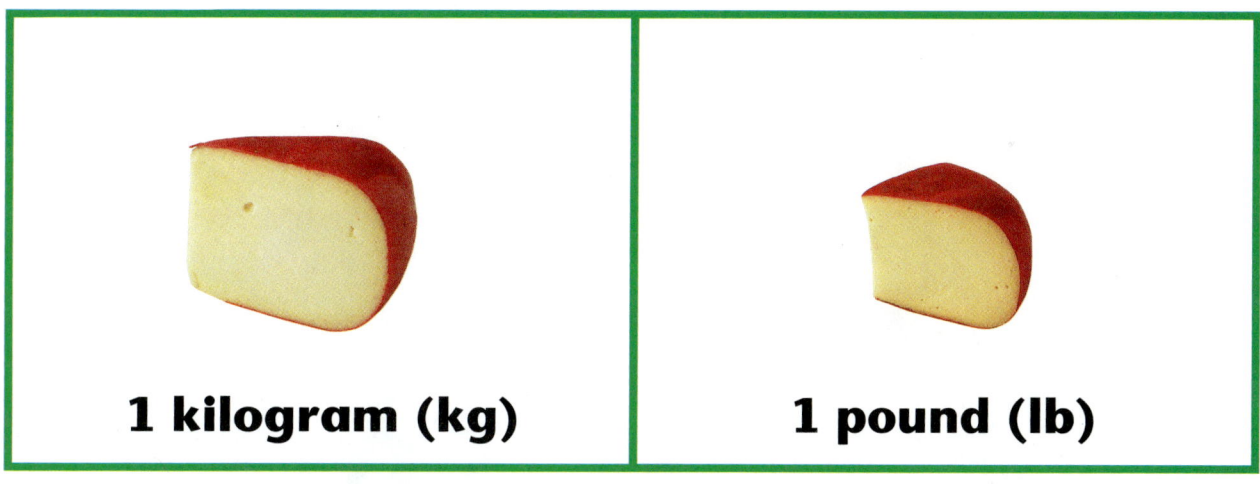

1 kilogram (kg) — 1 pound (lb)

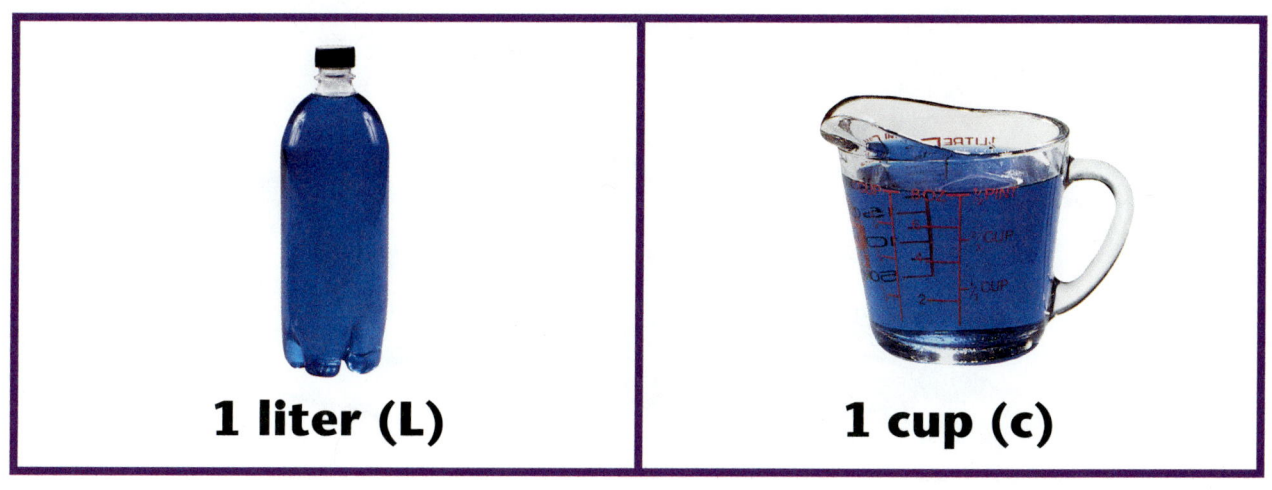

1 liter (L) — 1 cup (c)

Safety in Science

Here are some safety rules to follow when you do activities.

1. **Think ahead.** Study the steps and follow them.
2. **Be neat and clean.** Wipe up spills right away.
3. **Watch your eyes.** Wear safety goggles when told to do so.
4. **Be careful with sharp things.**
5. **Do not eat or drink things.**

 Visit the Multimedia Science Glossary to see illustrations of these words and to hear them pronounced. www.hspscience.com

Glossary

A glossary lists words in alphabetical order. To find a word, look it up by its first letter or letters.

adaptation

A body part or behavior that helps a living thing. (74)

amphibian

A kind of animal that has smooth, wet skin. (46)

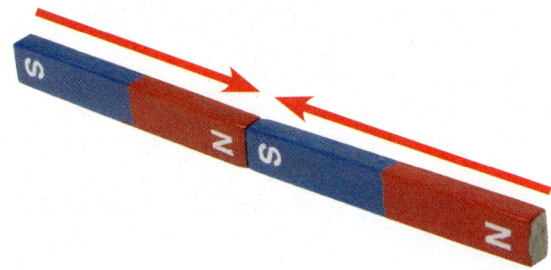

attract

To pull something. A magnet attracts things made of iron.

beach

Flat sandy land along a shore.

R27

Multimedia Science Glossary www.hspscience.com

bird

The only kind of animal that has feathers. (45)

camouflage

A kind of adaptation where an animal's color or pattern helps it hide. (78)

condense

To change from water vapor into tiny water drops. The drops form clouds. (44)

crater

A hole in a surface that is shaped like a bowl. The moon has many craters. (242)

desert

Land that gets very little rain.

dissolve

To completely mix a solid with a liquid. (115)

R28

Glossary

drought
A long time with little rain that causes the land to get very dry.

edible
Describes something that is safe to eat.

environment
All the things that are in a place. (68)

erosion
When moving water changes the land by carrying rocks and soil to new places.

evaporate
To change from liquid into water vapor. (180)

fall
The season after summer where the air begins to get cooler. (208)

R29

Multimedia Science Glossary www.hspscience.com

fish
A kind of animal that is covered in scales, uses gills to breathe, and lives in water. (47)

float
To stay on top of a liquid. (116)

flood
When rivers and streams get too full and the water flows onto land.

flowers
The part of a plant that makes fruits.

food chain
A diagram that shows how animals and plants are linked by what they eat. (86)

force
Something that makes an object move or stop moving.

Glossary

forest

Land that is covered with trees.

fruits

The parts of a plant that hold the seeds.

gas

A kind of matter that does not have its own shape. (123)

gills

The part of a fish that takes air from the water. (39)

gravity

A force that pulls things down to the ground.

habitat

The place where an animal finds food, water, and shelter.

R31

Multimedia Science Glossary www.hspscience.com

heat

A kind of energy that makes things hotter. (138)

hill

A high place that is smaller than a mountain and usually round on top.

humus

Pieces of dead plants and animals. Humus, clay, and sand make up soil.

inquiry skills

The skills people use to find out information. (12)

insect

A kind of animal that has three body parts and six legs. (48)

lake

A body of water with land all around it.

R32

Glossary

larva
Another name for a caterpillar. (54)

leaves
The parts of a plant that take in light and air to make food.

length
The measure of how long a solid is. (110)

life cycle
All the parts of a plant's or animal's life. (52)

light
A kind of energy that lets us see. (144)

liquid
A kind of matter that flows and takes the shape of its container. (114)

R33

Multimedia Science Glossary www.hspscience.com

living

Needing food, water, and air to grow and change. (32)

loudness

How loud or soft a sound is. (152)

lungs

The part of some animals that helps them breathe air. Pigs are animals that use lungs to breathe. (39)

magnet

An object that will attract things made of iron.

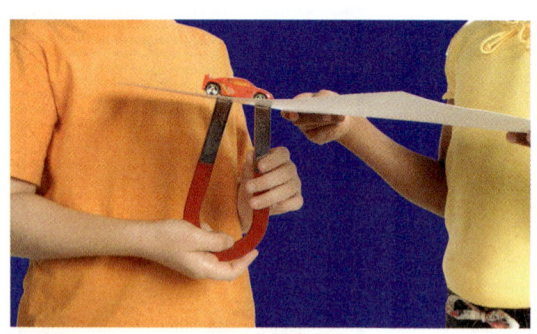

magnetic force

The pulling force of a magnet.

mammal

A kind of animal that has hair or fur and feeds its young milk. (44)

Glossary

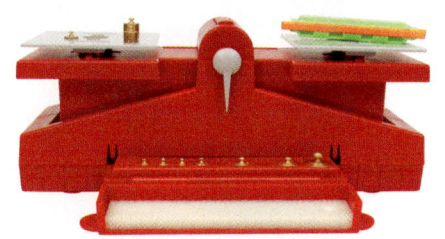

mass

The measure of how much matter something has. You can measure mass with a balance. (110)

matter

Everything around you. Matter can be a solid, liquid, or gas. (100)

migrate

To move to a new place to find food. (210)

mixture

Two or more things that have been mixed together. (108)

moon

A huge ball of rock in the sky that does not give off its own light. (229)

motion

When something is moving. Things are in motion when they move.

R35

Multimedia Science Glossary www.hspscience.com

mountain
The highest kind of land, with sides that slope toward the top.

natural resource
Anything from nature that people can use.

nonedible
Describes something that is not safe to eat.

nonliving
Not needing food, water, and air and not growing. (33)

nutrients
Minerals in the soil that plants need to grow and stay healthy.

ocean
A large body of salt water.

Glossary

oxygen

A kind of gas that plants give off and animals need to breathe. People need trees to get oxygen. (83)

pitch
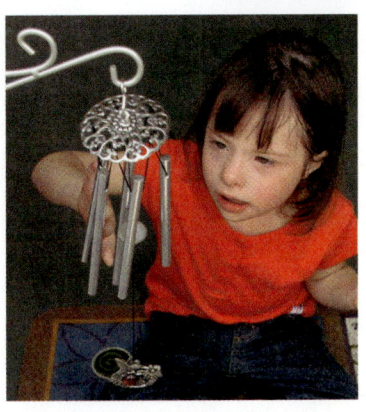
How high or low a sound is. (153)

plain

Flat land that spreads out a long way.

pole

Near an end of a magnet where the pull is strongest.

pollen

A powder that flowers need to make seeds. Bees help carry pollen from one flower to another. (84)

pollution

Waste that causes harm to land, water, or air.

Multimedia Science Glossary www.hspscience.com

pull

To tug an object closer to you.

pupa

The part of a life cycle where a caterpillar changes into a butterfly. (54)

push

To press an object away from you.

recycle

To use old resources to make new things.

reduce

To use less of a natural resource.

repel

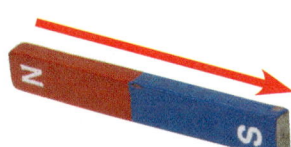

To push away. Poles that are the same on a magnet repel each other.

R38

Glossary

reptile
A kind of animal that has scaly, dry skin. (46)

reuse
To use a natural resource again.

river
A large body of moving water.

rock
A hard, nonliving thing that comes from Earth.

roots
The part of a plant that holds it in the soil and takes in water and nutrients.

rotate
To spin around like a top. Earth rotates and causes day and night. (234)

R39

Multimedia Science Glossary www.hspscience.com

S

science tools

The tools that help scientists find what they need. (20)

season

A season is a time of year. The seasons are spring, summer, fall, and winter. (194)

seed coat

A covering that protects a seed.

seeds

The parts of a plant that new plants grow from.

senses

The way we tell what the world is like. The five senses are sight, hearing, smell, taste, and touch. (4)

shadow

A dark place made when an object blocks light. (146)

R40

Glossary

shelter

A place where animals can be safe. (40)

sink

To fall to the bottom of a liquid. (117)

soil

The top layer of Earth, made of sand, humus, and clay.

solid

A kind of matter that keeps its shape. (107)

sound

A kind of energy that you hear. (150)

speed

The measure of how fast something moves.

spring
The season after winter where the weather gets warmer. (196)

star
An object in the sky that gives off its own light. (228)

steam
Gas that comes from boiling water. (126)

stem
The part of a plant that holds up the plant and lets food and water move through the plant.

stream
A small body of moving water that flows downhill.

summer
The season after spring that is usually hot. Summer has many hours of daylight. (202)

Glossary

sun

The star closest to Earth. (228)

sunlight

Light that comes from the sun.

tadpole

A young frog that comes out of an egg and has gills to breathe. (52)

temperature

The measure of how hot or cold something is. You can measure temperature with a thermometer. (174)

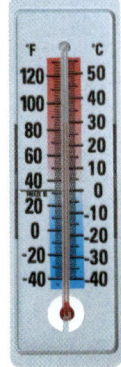

thermometer

A tool used to measure temperature. (174)

valley

The low land between mountains or hills.

R43

Multimedia Science Glossary www.hspscience.com

vibrate

To move quickly back and forth. (150)

water cycle

The movement of water from Earth to the air and back again. (180)

water vapor

Water in the air that you can not see. (180)

weather

What the air outside is like. (168)

winter

The season after fall that is usually cold. Winter has the fewest hours of daylight. (214)

R44

Index

A

Adaptations
   of animals, 76–77
   of plants, 74–75
Air, 122
   for animals, 39
Albuquerque International Balloon Fiesta, Albuquerque, New Mexico, 94
Alligator, 72
Amphibians, 46
Anemometer, 176
Animals
   adaptations of, 76–77
   bird, 45
   butterfly, 54–55
   camouflage, 78
   classifying, 44–48
   environment for, 68–69
   in fall, 210
   fish, 47
   in food chains, 86
   frog, 52–53
   growth and changes in, 52–56
   insects, 48
   as living things, 32
   mammals, 44
   needs of, 38–40
   plants helped by, 84–85
   plants used by, 82–83
   reptiles and amphibians, 46
   in spring, 198
   in summer, 204
   in winter, 216
Anteater, 76–77
Ants, 48

B

Apples, 206
Arctic fox, 78, 88, 89
Arm bones, R4
Asking questions, in investigating, 10
Astronauts, 242, 244–245

Balance, 22, 110, 118
Banyan tree, 74
Bar graphs, R22–R23
Bear, 86
Beaver, 82
Bee, 80
Beetle, 48
Bells, pitch of, 153
Birds, 45
   feathers of, 42, 45, 77
   shelter for, 40
Bison, 204
Blenders, 18
Blood, R9
Blood vessels, R9
Body, water in, 112
Bones, R4
Brain, R6
Breathing
   with gills, 39, 47
   by people, R3
Brushing teeth, R12–R13
Bubbles, biggest, 120
Butterflies, 48
   camouflage of, 78
   carrying pollen, 84
   life cycle of, 54–55
   monarch, 90

C

c (cup), R25
Calves, 60
Camouflage, 78, 89
Canada, 218
Caterpillars, 36, 54
Cause and effect, R16
C (Celsius) degrees, R25
Cell phones, 156–157
Celsius (C) degrees, R25
Centimeter (cm), R24
Centimeter (cm) ruler, R24
Circulatory system, R9
Cirrus clouds, 182
Classify
   animals, 43
   as inquiry skill, 12
   living and nonliving things, 31, 34
   matter, 99
   toys, 98
   See also Sorting
Cleanliness, R11
Clothing
   for astronauts, 244–245
   for winter, 214
Clouds, 182
   make, 179
   rain, 178
   from steam, 126
   in water cycle, 180
cm (centimeter), R24
Collecting data, R20
Color, heat and, 139, 221
Communicate
   daytime sky, 227

R45

as inquiry skill, 12
in investigating, 11
where animals live, 67
Compare
adult and young animals, 51
daily weather, 167
fruit, 19
as inquiry skill, 14
mass, 105
in reading, R15
seeds, 207
Contrast, in reading, R15
Cooling, 124–125
in summer, 204
Cows, 60
Craters, on moon, 238, 242
Crisp, Joy, 246
Cumulus clouds, 182
Cup (c), R25

Data, collecting, R20
Day, 232, 234–235
Daylight, 228
in fall, 208, 209
in spring, 196
in summer, 202
in winter, 214
Daytime sky, 228
Dead–leaf butterfly, 78
Deer, 82
Details (in reading), R14
Digestive system, R7
Dissolve, 115
Dog, 56, 85
Draw conclusions
fruit protection, 9
how animals hide, 73
how to stay warm, 213

as inquiry skill, 13
in investigating, 11
in reading, R18
about shadows, 143
Dropper, 21
Drum, 154

Eardrum, R2
Ears, R2
hearing, 4
Earth, rotation of, 234–236
Edison, Thomas Alva, 158
Elephants, 83
Energy
from foods, R7
heat, 138
light, 144
sound, 150
Environments, 68–70
Evaporation, 187
Evening, 236
Ewe and lambs, 198
Eyes, R1
sight, 4

Fahrenheit (F) degrees, R25
Fall, 195, 208
animals in, 210
plants in, 209
F (Fahrenheit) degrees, R25
Feathers (birds), 42, 45, 77
Fins, 77
Fire
heat from, 140
light from, 144
Fish, 39, 47, 78

Floating, 116–117
Flounder, 78
Flowers
food for bees from, 80
pollen of, 84
in spring, 197
Food
for animals, 38, 83, 210, 216
digestion of, R7
Food chain, 86
Forceps, 20
4–H Children's Garden, Michigan State University, 27
Foxes, 40
camouflage of, 78, 88, 89
Friction, heat from, 140
Frog, 46
camouflage of, 78
life cycle of, 52–53
Fruit
comparing, 19
in fall, 209
protection for, 9
Full moon, 241
Fur, of mammals, 44

Gases
observing, 122–123
steam, 126
in sun, 136
Gecko, 46
Geese, 198, 210
Gills, 39, 47
Giraffe, 38
Goldfish, 77
Goslings, 198
Graphs, 221, R22–R23
Griffiths, Emma, 90

Index

Guitar strings, 150, 151
Gums, R12

Hair (mammals), 44
Hand lens, 20
Health habits, R10–R13
Hearing, 4, R2
Heart, R9
Heat and heating, 138–139
    of matter, 124–125
    sources of, 140
    from the sun, 137
Heron, 82
Hip bones, R4
Holly, 215
Honey possum, 84
Hummingbird, 75
Hypothesize
    as inquiry skill, 13
    in investigating, 10
    plants and light, 193
    watching sound, 149

Inner ear, R2
Inquiry skills, 12–16
    classify, 12
    communicate, 12
    compare, 14
    draw conclusions, 125
Igloos, 218–219
In. (inches), R24
Inches (in.), R24
Inch (in.) ruler, R24
Infer
    clouds, 179
    hot–weather activities, 201
    as inquiry skill, 16
    matter in a bottle, 121
    surface of the moon, 239
    draw conclusions, 13
    hypothesize, 13
    infer, 16
    make a model, 13
    measure, 14
    observe, 15
    plan an investigation, 16
    predict, 15
    sequence, 14
Insects, 48
Insta–Lab
    act out summer activities, 203
    cold–weather clothes, 215
    compare living things, 33
    environments near you, 69
    homes from plants, 83
    how far will it roll?, 16
    how many legs?, 48
    light and dark, 139
    make mixtures, 109
    matter up close, 101
    moon changes, 241
    moonlight, 229
    new leaves, 197
    observe beaks, 77
    observing weather, 169
    pet food survey, 39
    straw instruments, 153
    swim!, 209
    things seem to move, 236
    what can light pass through?, 145
    what do you hear?, 5
    what floats?, 117
    where's the heat?, 175
    wind hunt, 123
Intestines, R7
Inuit, 218–219
Investigate, 10–12
    animal homes, 37
    animals grow and change, 51
    animals in a tree, 81
    classify animals, 43
    classify matter, 99
    compare fruit, 19
    compare seeds, 207
    daily weather, 167
    daytime sky, 227
    fruit protection, 9
    heat from the sun, 137
    hot weather activities, 201
    how senses work, 3
    how to stay warm, 213
    as inquiry skill, 16
    living and nonliving things, 31
    make clouds, 179
    matter in a bottle, 121
    measure temperature, 173
    measuring mass, 105
    model day and night, 233
    plants and light, 193
    shadows, 143
    shape of liquids, 113
    some animals hide, 73
    surface of the moon, 239
    watching sound, 149
    where animals live, 67
Iris (eye), R1

Jade plant, 74
Jaguar, 66
Jet, 152

R47

Kilogram (kg), R25

L (liters). See Liters
Lamps
    heat from, 140
    light from, 144
Larva, 54
lb (pound), R25
Leaves
    in fall, 209
    in winter, 215
Leg bones, R4
Length, 110
    measuring, 22
Life cycle, 52
    of butterflies, 54–55
    of frogs, 52–53
Light, 144–145
    from moon, 229
    for plants, 193
    and shadows, 146
    from stars, 226
    from sun, 228 (See also Daylight)
Light bulbs, 158
Lion, 76
Liquids
    floating and sinking, 116–117
    mixtures of, 115
    observing, 114
    oil, 128
    shape of, 113
Liters (L), R25
Living things, 32
    classifying, 34
    environments of, 68
    needs of, 34
    See also Animals; Plants
Lizard, 46
Loudness, 152
Louisiana Children's Museum, New Orleans, Louisiana, 95
Lumpkin, Ivy, 220
Lungs
    of animals, 39
    of people, R8

Magnifying box, 20
Mailboxes, lighted, 220
Main idea, R14
Make a model
    of day and night, 233
    as inquiry skill, 13
Mammals, 44
Maple seeds, 75
Maple sugaring, 162
Maple trees, 209
Marquez Sanchez, Manuel, 130
Mars, 230, 246
Mass, 110
    measuring, 22, 105
Math in science
    measurements, R24–R25
    using tables, charts, and graphs, R20–R23
Matter, 100–101
    classify, 99
    gases, 122–123
    heating and cooling, 124–125
    liquids, 114–117
    solids, 106–110
    sorting, 102
Measure, R24–R25
    as inquiry skill, 14
    liquids, 113
    mass, 105
    rain, 175
    science tools for, 21–22
    solids, 110
    temperature, 173, 174
    wind, 176
Measuring cup, 21, 118
Measuring tape, 22
Middle ear, R2
Migrate, 210
Milk cartons, 130
Mixtures
    of liquid, 115
    of solids, 108–109
Monarch butterflies, 90
Moon, 229
    changes in shape of, 240–241
    craters on, 238, 242
    exploring, 242
Morning, 236
Mountains, 33
Mouth, R7, R8
Muscles, R5, R9
Muscular system, R5
Musical instruments, 154

Nerves, R6
Nervous system, R6
New moon, 241
Night, 232, 234–235
Nighttime sky, 229
    moon in, 240–241
Nonliving things, 33

Index

classifying, 34
in environments, 69
Noon, 236
North Country Planetarium, Plattsburgh State University, 163
Nose, R3, R8
smell, 4

Observe
animal homes, 37
animals in a tree, 81
gases, 122–123
as inquiry skill, 15
in investigating, 10
liquids, 114
sky, 228–229
solids, 106–107
Oil spills, 128–129
Outer ear, R2
Owls, 40
Oxygen, from plants, 83

Panda, 38
Patterns
camouflage, 78
moon shapes, 240–241
Peacock, 45
People in Science
Joy Crisp, 246
Thomas Alva Edison, 158
Emma Griffiths, 90
Ivy Lumpkin, 220
Manuel Marquez Sanchez, 130
Chloe Ruiz, 60

Bob Stokes, 186
Picture graphs, R23
Pig, 204
Pineapple, 8
Pitch (sound), 153, 159
Plan a fair test, 11
Plan an investigation
heat from the sun, 137
as inquiry skill, 16
Planets, 229
Mars, 246
Plants
adaptations of, 74–75
environments for, 68–69
in fall, 209
in food chains, 86
helped by animals, 84–85
light for, 193
as living things, 32, 33
in spring, 197
in summer, 203
used by animals, 82–83
in winter, 215
Polar bear, 50
Pollen, 84
Porcupine, 77
Pound (lb), R25
Precipitation, 181
Predict
how senses work, 3
as inquiry skill, 15
Pupa, 54, 55
Pupil (eyes), R1

Quarter moon, 240, 241

Radios, cell phones as, 156
Rain, 186
measuring, 175
in spring, 196, 197
in water cycle, 181
Rainbow trout, 86
Rain clouds, 178
Rain gauge, 175
Reading in science
cause and effect, R16
compare and contrast, R15
draw conclusions, R18
main idea and details, R14
sequence, R17
summarize, R19
Recording data, R21
Red soldier fish, 47
Reptiles, 46
Respiratory system, R8
Robot rovers (Mars), 246
Rocks
from moon, 242
as nonliving things, 32, 33
Rose, 75
Rotate (Earth), 234–236
Ruiz, Chloe, 60
Ruler, 22, 110

Safety, 6
in science, R26
weather, 187
Sailfish, 47
Satellites, weather, 185
Saxophone, 154

R49

Scarlet ibis, 76
Science projects
　animals and their young, 61
　cool colors, 221
　evaporation, 187
　explore cooling, 131
　favorite season graphs, 221
　foods birds eat, 61
　mixtures all around, 131
　moon journal, 247
　pitch, 159
　sun catcher, 159
　warm or cool, 247
　watch plants change, 91
　weather safety, 187
　what makes seeds stick, 91
Science tools, 20–22
　telescopes, 230
Science Up Close
　animals and their young, 56
　camouflage, 78
　musical instruments, 154
　seasons, 194–195
　telescopes, 230
　what is steam?, 126
Sea lion caves, Oregon, 26
Seals, 44
Seashells, 200
Seasons, 194–195
　fall, 208–210
　spring, 196–198
　summer, 202–204
　winter, 214–216
Sea turtles, 58–59
Seeds
　carried by animals, 85
　comparing, 207
Senses, 4–6, R1–R3
　taste buds, 2

Sequence
　as inquiry skill, 14
　in reading, R17
Shadows, 142, 143, 146
Shape of liquids, 113
Sheep, 198
Shelter
　for animals, 40
　igloos, 218–219
Sight, 4
Sinking, 116–117
Skeletal system, R4
Skin, R3
　touch, 4
Skull, R4
Sky
　during day, 228
　moving objects in, 236
　during night, 229
　observing, 228–229
Smart spacesuits, 244–245
Smell, 4, R3
Snow, 214
　igloos from, 218–219
　in water cycle, 181
Snowflakes, 219
Soap, 114
Solids
　measuring, 110
　mixing, 108–109
　observing, 106–107
Sorting, 102. **See also Classify**
Sounds
　differences among, 152–153
　how sounds are made, 150–151
　of musical instruments, 154
　travel of, 148
　watching, 149

Space station, 244
Spacesuits, 244–245
Spine, R4
Spring, 194–196
　animals in, 198
　plants in, 192, 197
　water in, 125
Spring Maple–Sugaring Festival, Massachusetts, 162
Squashes, 209
Squirrel, 85, 210
Stampede Pass, Washington, 219
Stars, 228, 229
　light from, 226
Steam, 126
Stokes, Bob, 186
Stomach, R7
Stoneflies, 86
Stoves, heat from, 140
Stratus clouds, 182
Straw instruments, 153
Summarize, in reading, R19
Summer, 195, 202
　animals in, 204
　plants in, 203
　water in, 124
Sun, 228
　gases in, 136
　heat from, 137, 138
　in water cycle, 180
Sun catcher, 159
Sunlight, 144

T

Tables, R20–R21
Tachi, Susumu, 89
Tadpoles, 52, 53

Index

Tally charts/tables, R21
Taste, 4, R3
Taste buds, 2
Technology
    cell phones, 156–157
    cleaning up oil, 128–129
    hiding things, 88–89
    igloos, 218–219
    sea turtle travel, 58–59
    smart spacesuits, 244–245
    weather, 184–185
Teeth
    of animals, 77
    caring for, R12–R13
Telescope, 230
Temperature, measure, 173, 174, R25
Test, in investigating, 11
Thermometers, 21, 174
Thorns (on plants), 75
Thunderstorm, 186, 202
Tiger, 44
Tomato plant, 203
Tongues
    of animals, 77
    taste, 4
    taste buds on, 2
Touch, 4
Trees
    in fall, 209
    in spring, 197
    in summer, 202
    in winter, 212, 215
Trumpet, 154
Turtle, 46, 58–59

United States, day and night in, 232, 234, 235

Vibrate, 150
Violin, 154

Water
    for animals, 38
    in body, 112
    as liquid, 114
    as nonliving thing, 33
    steam, 126
    in summer, 124
    in winter, 125
Water cycle, 180–181
Water pollution, 128
Water vapor, 180
Weather, 168–169
    changes in, 184–185
    clothing and activities for, 170
    clouds, 182
    in fall, 208
    inches of snow vs. rain, 166
    in spring, 196
    in summer, 202
    water cycle, 180–181
    in winter, 214
Weather patterns, 167
Weather safety, 187
Weather vanes, 176
Weight, measuring, 22
Whispers, 152
Wind, 123
    measuring, 176
Wind chimes, pitch of, 153
Windsock, 176
Wings, 76
Winter, 195, 214
    animals in, 216
    plants in, 215
    trees in, 212
    water in, 125
Wolf, 32

Zebra, 38

Photograph Credits
Page Placement Key: (t) top; (b) bottom; (c) center; (l) left; (r) right; (bg) background; (fg) foreground; (i) inset.

Page Placement Key: (t) top; (b) bottom; (c) center; (l) left; (r) right; (bg) background; (fg) foreground; (i) inset.

Cover: (front) Paul Nicklen/National Geographic/Getty Images; (back) Robert & Lorri Franz/Corbis; (back) (bg) Rosemary Calvert/Getty Images.

Front End Sheets: Page 1, (t) Alaska Stock Images; bg) Alaska Stock Images; Page 2, (t), (b) David W. Hamilton/Getty Images; (bg) Alaska Stock Images; Page 3, (t) Alaska Stock Images; (b) Joel Sartore/National Geographic/Getty Images; (bg) Alaska Stock Images.

Title Page: Paul Nicklen/National Geographic/Getty Images.

Copyright Page: (inset) Paul Nicklen/National Geographic/Getty Images; (bg) Rosemary Calvert/Getty Images.

Table of Contents: iv Gay Bumgarner/Stone/Getty Images; vi Johnny Johnson/Photographer's Choice/Getty Images.

Back End Sheets: Page 1, (t) Thomas Mangelsen/Minden Pictures; (b) Norbert Rosing/National Geographic/Getty Images; (bg) Alaska Stock Images; Page 2, (t) Yva Momatiuk/John Eastcott/Minden Pictures; (c) Paul Nicklen/National Geographic/Getty Images; (b) Alaska Stock Images; (bg) Alaska Stock Images; Page 3, (t) Klein/Hubert/Peter Arnold, Inc.; (b) Theo Allofs/Visuals Unlimited; (bg) Alaska Stock Images.

Unit 1: viii Albuquerque International Balloon Fiesta, 1 Philip Gould/CORBIS; 28-29 Photodisc Green/Getty; 36 Alamy Images; (bg) Dave G. Houser/Corbis; 38 Jose Luis Pelaez, Inc./Corbis; 39 Jose Luis Pelaez, Inc./Corbis; 54 (l) Craig Hammell/Corbis, (r) Francisco Cruz/Superstock; 54-55 Corbis; 56-57 Getty Images; 57 Getty Images; 60 Andy Levin/Photo Researchers; 61 Craig Aurness/Corbis; 62 Lester Lefkowitz/Corbis; 63 (bg) Digital Vision(Royalty-free)/Getty Images; 65 (both) Getty Images; 66-67 Ariel Skelley/Corbis; 68 "Courtesy NASA/JPL-Caltech"; 70 Doug Stamm/Stammphoto.com; 72 (cl) Royalty-Free Corbis, (bl) Michael Newman/Photo Edit; 73 Royalty-Free Corbis; 78 (t) Workbookstock.com, (b) Mark Gibson Stock Photography; 80 Tom & Dee Ann McCarthy/Corbis; 84 (t) David Young-Wolff/Photo Edit; 84-85 Scott Barrow, Inc./SuperStock; 85 (br) Eduardo Garcia/Getty Images; 86 (tl) Spencer Grant/Photo Edit, (tr) Photodisc Blue/Getty Images, (bl) Spencer Grant/Photo Edit; 88 Asia Images/Getty; 89 Getty Images: 90 (t) Bettmann/Corbis, (b) Bettmann/Corbis; 92 (tc) Michael Newman/Photo Edit, (b) Gibson Stock Photography; 93 Tony Freeman/Photo Edit.

Unit 2: 94 Jonathan Blair/CORBIS; 95 AP/Wide World Photos; 96-97 Michael Deyoung/Age Fotostock; 98 Getty Images; 100 (t) Mark Polott/Index Stock Imagery, (b) William Manning/Corbis; 100-101 (bg) Leng/Leng/Corbis; 101 Craig Tuttle/Corbis; 102 (bg) Digital Vision, (bl) Royalty-free/Corbis; 103 Mark Polott/Index Stock Imagery; 107 Workbookstock.com; 108 (t) Jeff Greenberg/Index Stock Imagery, (c) Tony Freeman/PhotoEdit; 110 Jim Reed/Corbis; 114 (t) Royalty-free/Corbis, (c) Jonathan Nourok/PhotoEdit, (b) Royalty-Free/Corbis; 115 Royalty-free/Corbis; 116 (t) AP/Wide World Photos, (b) NASA; 118 Courtesy of the Weather Channel; 119 (bg) Bruce Peebles/Corbis; 121 (tl) Tony Freeman/PhotoEdit, (br) Jeff Greenberg/Index Stock Imagery; 122-123 Stephen Wilkes/Getty Images; 127 (all) Matheisi/Taxi/Getty Images; 128 (t) Richard Hutchings/PhotoEdit; (b) Bob Thomas/Stone/Getty Images; 129 (inset) Eric Cricton/Corbis, Pat O'Hara/CORBIS; 130 (t) ColorPic, Inc.; (b) Royalty-Free/CORBIS; 131 (c) Bob Thomas/Getty Images; 132 Network Productions/The Image Works; 134 (l) Photomondo/Getty Images; 135 (inset) Christi Carter/Grand Heilman Photography; Alamy Images; 136 (t) Digital Vision/Getty Images; (b) Phil Schermeister/CORBIS; 137 Christi Carter/Grant Heilman Photography; 138 David Allen Brandt/Stone/Getty Images; 140 (t) James Frank/Alamy Images; (b) Journal Courier/The Image Works; 141 (inset) John Colwell/Grant Heilman Photography; Robert Estall/CORBIS; 142 (t) Florian Moellers/Age Fotostock; (b) Chase Swift/CORBIS; 144 Murray Lee/Age Fotostock; 146 (t) James Frank/Alamy Images; (b) Robert Frerck/Odyssey/Chicago; 147 (inset) Eric and David Hosking/CORBIS; Werner Dieterich/Getty Images; 148 (t) Joseph Van Os/The Image Bank/Getty Images; (b) Royalty- Free/CORBIS; 149 (c) James Frank/Alamy Images; 150 (tr) Susan Findlay/Master file, (cl) B&C Alexander/Photo Researchers Inc., (r) Alan Fortune/Animals Animals, 151 B&C Alexander/Photo Researchers; 152 Courtesy The Lumpkin Family; 153 (bg) W. Cody/Corbis; 154 (tr) David Allen Brandt/Stone/Getty Images; (b) Robert Frerck/Odyssey/Chicago; 156-157 Astrofoto/Peter Arnold, Inc.; 158 Creative Concept/Index Stock Imagery; 160 Getty Images; 161 Roger Ressmeyer/Corbis; 162 Stocktrek/Corbis; 163 (c) G. Kalt/Masterfile; 164 Corbis; 292 Getty Images; 167 Zefa Visual Media - Germany/Index Stock Imagery; 170 Corbis; 172 Larry Landolfi/Photo Researchers; 172-173 Rev. Ronald Royer/Science Photo Library/Photo Researchers; 173 (t), (c) Larry Landolfi/Photo Researchers; (b) Eckhard Slawik/Photo Researchers; 174 (bg) NASA/Photo Researchers, (l) Bettmann/Corbis, (r) NASA/Photo Researchers; 175 (c) 1966 Corbis; Original image courtesy of NASA/Corbis; 176 NASA; 177 NASA; 178 (t) NASA; (c) AP/Wide World Photos; (b) NASA/JPC/Cornell; 181 (tl), (cl) Larry Landolfi/Photo Researchers, (tr) Eckhard Slawik/Photo Researchers; 181 (cr) Larry Landolfi/Photo Researchers; (b) Alamy Images.

Unit 3: 182 Tom and Pat Leeson; 183 Dr. Norm Lownds, Curator, 4-H Children's Garden; 184-185 Randy Wells/Corbis; 188-189 Getty Images; 190 (tl) Getty Images, (cl) A. & S. Carey/Masterfile, (bl) Paul Zahl/National Geographic Image Collection, (tr) Gary Thomas Sutto/Corbis, (cr) Getty Images, (br) Royalty-Free/Corbis; 191 (tl) Getty Images; 192 Michael & Patricia Fogden/Corbis; 194 (t) China Span/Animals Animals/Earth Scenes; (b) Winifred Wisniewski/Frank Lane Picture Agency/Corbis; 195 Kristian Cabanis/Age Fotostock; 196 (b) D. Robert & Lorri Franz/Corbis, (t) W. Perry Conway/Corbis; 197 D. Robert & Lorri Franz/Corbis; 198 Fritz Poelking/Age Fotostock; 200 (t) David Tipling/Nature Picture Library, (b) Tom Brakefield/Corbis; 201 (t) Robert Lubeck/Animals Animals/Earth Scenes, (b) John W. Bova/Photo Researchers, 202 (t) Darrell Gulin/Corbis, (c) Santiago Fernandez/Age Fotostock, (t) Marian Bacon/Animals Animals/Earth Scenes; 203 (t) Getty Images, (i) National Geographic/Getty Images, (b) Avi Klapfer/SeaPics.com; 204 (t) Paul Eekhoff/Masterfile, (c) IFA/eStock Photo/PictureQuest, (b) Jim Sugar/Corbis; 205 John W. Bova/Photo Researchers; 206 Norbert Rosing/National Geographic Image Collection; 208 (t) James Frank/Alamy Images; (b) Journal Courier/The Image Works; 209 (fg) John Colwell/Grant Heilman Photography; (bg) Robert Estall/CORBIS; 210 (all) E.R. Degginger/Color-Pic; 210-211 E.R. Degginger/Color-Pic; 211 (all) E.R. Degginger/Color-Pic; 213 (t) (all) E.R. Degginger/Color-Pic, (c) Gary Meszaros/Photo Researchers; 214 (t) Dr. Kenneth Lohmann/University of North Carolina, (b) Hamman Heldring of Animals Animals/Earth Scenes, 215 (t) John Pontier/Animals Animals/Earth Scenes, (b) Dr. Kenneth Lohmann/University of North Carolina; 216 Annie Griffiths/Corbis; 217 (bg) PictureQuest; 218 (tl) Robert Lubeck/Animals Animals/Earth Scenes, (tlc) Paul Eekhoff/Masterfile, (trc) Tom Brakefield/Corbis; (tr) Avi Klapfer/SeaPics.com; (b) (all) E.R. Degginger/Color-Pic; 219 (r) John Staples, Cordaly Photo Library Ltd./Corbis; 220-221 National Geographic/Getty Images, 222 William Ervin/Photo Researchers; 224-225 Patti Murray/Animals Animals/Earth Scenes, 226 Getty Images; 227 (t) Patti Murray/Animals Animals/Earth Scenes; 228 Kevin Leigh/Index Stock Imagery; 230 (t) Alamy Images, (b) Alamy Images; 231 (t) Niall Benvie/Corbis, (bl) Francois Gohier/Photo Researchers; 232 (bg) T. Allofs/Zefa, (t) Roland Seitre/Peter Arnold, Inc., (c) Norman Owen Tomalin/Bruce Coleman, Inc.; 233 (l) Alamy Images, (r) ABPL Image Library/Animals Animals/Earth Scenes; 234 (tl) Yva Momatiuk/John Eastcott/Minden Pictures, (tr) Tom Walker/Visuals Unlimited, (bl) Seapics.com, (bc) Ken Thomas/Photo Researchers, (br) Bernard Photo Productions/Animals Animals/Earth Scenes; 236 John Vucci/Peter Arnold, Inc.; 238 (t) Galen Rowell/Corbis, (bl) Alamy Images, (br) Bruce Coleman, Inc.; 239 McDonald Wildlife Photography/Animals Animals/Earth Scenes; 240 (l) Jonathan Blair/National Geographic Image Collection, Wild & Natural/Animals Animals/Earth Scenes; 241 (t) Eric and David Hosking/Corbis, John Pontier/Animals Animals/Earth Scenes; 243 (t) John Vucci/Peter Arnold, Inc.; 244 AFP/Getty; 246 (t) Stephen Dunn/The Hartford Courant, (b) Scott Camazine/Photo Researchers; 247 (bg) Creatas Royalty Free Stock Resources.

Glossary: R27 ABPL Image Library/Animals Animals/Earth Scenes; R27 John W. Bova/Photo Researchers; R27 Marian Bacon/Animals Animals/Earth Scenes; R28 (c) 1966 Corbis; original image courtesy of NASA/Corbis; R28 Andrew Brown; Ecoscene/Corbis; R28 Mary Ellen Bartley/Picture Arts/Corbis; R28 Royalty-free/Corbis; R28 Yva Momatiuk/John Eastcott/Minden Pictures; R29 Avi Klapfer/SeaPics.com; R29 Michael P. Gadomski/Photo Researchers; R29 Patti Murray/Animals Animals/Earth Scenes; R29 Photodisc Red (Royalty-Free)/Getty Images; R30 Alamy Images; R30 Bill Ross/Corbis; R30 Grant Heilman/Grant Heilman Photography; R31 Craig K. Lorenz/Photo Researchers; R31 Gregory W. Brown/Animals Animals/Earth Scenes; R31 Patrik Giardino/Corbis; R31 Royalty-free/Corbis; R32 Barry Runk/Grant Heilman Photography; R32 E.R. Degginger/Color-Pic; R32 Gary Meszaros/Photo Researchers; R32 Gregory K. Scott/Photo Researchers; R32 IFA/eStock Photo/PictureQuest; R32 John Mitchell/Photo Researchers; R33 John Staples, Cordaly Photo Library, Ltd./Corbis; R33 Paul Zahl/National Geographic Image Collection; R33 Scott Barrow, Inc./Superstock; R34 Bob Gelberg/Masterfile; R34 Rev. Ronald Royer/Science Photo Library/Photo Researchers; R34 Usher/Premium Stock/PictureQuest/Jupiter Images; R35 Alamy Images; R35 Dana Hursey/Masterfile; R35 Gary Thomas Sutto/Corbis; R35 Liz Barry/Lonely Planet Images; R36 E.R. Degginger/Color-Pic; R36 John Vucci/Peter Arnold, Inc.; R37 David Young-Wolff/PhotoEdit; R37 Getty Images; R38 Digital Vision (RF)/Getty Images; R38 Jerome Wexler/Photo Researchers; R38 Visuals Unlimited; R39 Jose Luis Pelaez, Inc./Corbis; R39 Mark Gibson Stock Photography; R39 W. Perry Conway/Corbis; R40 Creative Concept/Index Stock Imagery; R40 Getty Images; R40 Peter Walton/Index Stock Imagery; R40 Photodisc Blue (Royalty-free)/Getty Images; R41 Freeman Patterson/Masterfile; R41 Getty Images; R41 John Mitchell/Photo Researchers; R42 Royalty-Free/Corbis.

All other photos © Harcourt School Publishers. Harcourt photographers; Weronica Ankarorn, Eric Camden, Doug Dukane, Ken Kinzie, April Riehm, and Steve Williams.